The Political Philosophy
of the New Deal

The
POLITICAL
PHILOSOPHY
of the
NEW
DEAL

Hubert H. Humphrey

LOUISIANA STATE UNIVERSITY PRESS
Baton Rouge 1970

Copyright © 1970 by Hubert H. Humphrey
All rights reserved

Library of Congress Catalog Card Number 71–122356
ISBN 0–8071–0528–7

Manufactured in the United States of America
Designed by A. R. Crochet

Foreword

THE REACTION of many persons to the New Deal between 1930 and 1940 was similar to the sentiments evoked in the young William Wordsworth by the initial stages of the French Revolution, of which he later wrote, "Bliss was it in that dawn to be alive, / But to be young was very heaven." In 1939, though older than his fellow graduate students at Louisiana State University, Hubert Humphrey was young, strenuously and joyously alive, and almost in very heaven, because he was studying politics and government in preparation for what would undoubtedly have been a brilliant literary career in scholarship and teaching. In addition he held a teaching assistantship which carried the munificent remuneration of $400 and free tuition in an age which had not witnessed "the revolution of rising expectations" among graduate students. More important to him than any material rewards was the opportunity not only to study and to learn, but also to teach a section of a course in American government, a task to which he brought zeal, energy, and originality.

That Hubert Humphrey was a graduate student of the highest quality is shown by the official records of Louisiana State University. What the formal records do not show and can never reveal is that he approached his studies with a merry heart and a sense of personal involvement in public affairs. Where some students brought drudgery or pedantry to the performance of their assigned work, Hubert Humphrey brought gaiety, imagination, and a sense of purpose. To him knowledge was good not only for its own sake but as something to be used for the attainment of desirable ends. Accordingly, his thesis for the Master of Arts degree, written under the supervision of Professor A. B. Daspit, is not an objective essay in the usual academic sense. Indeed, the essay is infused with the writer's underlying assumptions concerning the nature of society, the ends and purposes of government, and the rights of man which he has continued to hold with a singular degree of consistency during his public career.

In his master's essay, Hubert Humphrey's commitment to the indigenous traditions of American democracy is evident throughout. Liberty occupies a high place in his scheme of values, but liberty is more than freedom from governmental restraint. It is also freedom from all arbitrary power, economic and social. Private property is a positive good, so good indeed that everyone should have some of it. Equality is an end to be pursued particularly with respect to the opportunity of each individual person to develop to his full capacity his physical, intellectual, and moral qualities. There is, therefore, an abiding faith in the inherent moral worth and dignity of the individual person and at the same time a conviction that individual interests can and must be protected and promoted by community action. Accordingly, his stress upon individual happiness is never separated from the interests of the community.

Altogether Hubert Humphrey's political ideas as a graduate student were characterized by a progressive temper and an optimistic and tolerant outlook. Except for his firm commitment to the basic tenets of the American political tradition, he approached the study of politics with a flexible and practical mind. Hence he was suspicious of doctrinaires and any fixed ideas concerning issues of public policy and and was at all times aware of compromise as a cohesive force in representative government. Although he had a buoyant confidence in the ability of reasonable men by taking thought to improve the world, he knew that reasonable men may disagree and he was ever willing to put his thoughts to the test of argumentative combat. In expounding his views he had a zest for the mobilization of facts to support them and a boldness in the advancement of novel and at times unpopular applications of older ideas. He was impatient with clinging to the old just because it was old, but he equally rejected ideas which were only superficially novel.

Hubert Humphrey's departure from the academic profession represented a net loss to it in terms of scholarship, zealous teaching, and gaiety, but his entry into public life has been a net gain to the American republic. He has brought to public affairs the same qualities of character and intellect which he had as a student. Equally important, as a statesman he has continued to be an educator in an area where the task is more difficult than that of campus and classroom and where the rewards for success and penalties for failure are substantially greater. It is the good fortune of all America that in his special way this man has continued to study, learn, and joyously teach.

ROBERT J. HARRIS

Charlottesville, Virginia

Preface

MORE THAN ANYTHING ELSE, the New Deal was a change in the scope of public responsibility, particularly in the spheres of economic and social action. As such, it was philosophic father to the Fair Deal, to the New Frontier, and to the whole host of landmark legislative enactments of the mid-1960's which compose the Great Society.

It is some three decades since I began the research for this master's thesis on the New Deal, and the intervening years have not diluted my respect or admiration for the farsighted and visionary legislative direction President Franklin Roosevelt established for our nation.

Though contemporary events affect earlier interpretation and hindsight—as always—generates new wisdom and comprehension, I still feel much affection for this material from the pen of my younger self and I am pleased that the Louisiana State University Press has asked to publish this thesis.

My affection for the New Deal is by no means confined to nostalgia. I think there are some sound lessons for today in President Roosevelt's activist political judgments.

Franklin Roosevelt brought government to the people. He personalized the role of government and brought better understanding of that social contract so vital for a democracy—the direct relationships of the people to their government and the government to the people. This conception of government and the people has continued—and today people look to the presidency more than ever as the people's office and the central force in political affairs.

The New Deal added a new dimension to modern liberalism. The liberal of the Populist period saw government as an umpire in the contest between powerful interests and the people. The nineteenth-century liberal saw the role of government as restraining and curbing the abuses of power. The New Deal made liberalism a positive force for the betterment of the human condition; it saw freedom as more than the absence of restraint. Freedom was characterized by a better life, better homes, better education. Government was to be more than the protector and the regulator, it was to be a partner, a constructive force, in improving the nation and helping the individual.

The underlying premise of the New Deal—I quote from Franklin Roosevelt—that "the legitimate object of government is to do for the people what needs to be done but which they cannot by individual effort do at all or do as well for themselves"—is as valid today as when first articulated.

The 1930's were difficult days for our nation, but these are also trying times.

These times are difficult for those who seek to save man from the perils of the arms race, and from the threat of further confrontations between nations.

These are difficult times for the managers of our national economy, and for those who are responsible for the strength and vitality of our cities.

These are difficult days for those who believe in an open society and in the equality of man.

I hope this examination of the New Deal—a philosophy of government designed for difficult days—may prove useful and instructive for those who take seriously the art of politics today.

HUBERT H. HUMPHREY

St. Paul, Minnesota
1970

Acknowledgment

The author wishes to acknowledge his indebtedness to Professor A. B. Daspit, under whom this thesis was written, and to the other members of the Department of Government of Louisiana State University who gave so freely of their time in consultation and advice.

Contents

Introduction

MARCH 4, 1933, Franklin D. Roosevelt was inaugurated as President of the United States. Before midnight on March 5, 1933, the German Reichstag had placed absolute power into the hands of Adolf Hitler. Those twenty-four hours may well be recorded as the most eventful period in world history. Eight years later these two men stood as symbols of two opposing ways of life, as representatives of two conflicting ideologies. Hitler and his Nazi cohorts had placed the death blow to the German Weimar Republic. Roosevelt and his administration had dedicated themselves to adapting existing economic organizations to the service of the people—all to be accomplished within the procedure of democratic institutions.

It is certain that Mr. Roosevelt did not envisage the present situation on March 4, 1933. The far-reaching plans of the New Deal administration were not to be performed with artillery, tanks, and bombing planes. It is entirely possible that he was aware of the possibility of war, but, like most Americans, he rejected war as an instrument of national policy. It was a calamity to be avoided, not an opportunity to be studied and desired. The New Deal was essentially a peace program. It was an effort to regain and expand economic and political liberty. The experimentation and planning so vitally necessary were dependent upon a world at peace. The moment the threat of war overshadowed the land, New Deal programs had to be held in abeyance. In May, 1940, the philosophy of the Commonwealth Club speech was set aside, and the nation girded itself for war.

During the last half-century America has witnessed three political reform movements abruptly checked by the impact of war. Populism subsided with the jingoism of the Spanish-American conflict. Theodore Roosevelt's Bull Moose movement and the New Freedom of Woodrow Wilson were stifled by World War I. The New Deal, already losing its forward surge by 1938, has been brought to a standstill by the present world conflict.

We may well ask ourselves, what will be the effect of this latest conflict on New Deal accomplishments? Has the New Deal revitalized the faith in democracy of the one-third "ill-housed, ill-fed and ill-clothed"? If so, then the program, while planned for a peacetime economy, may have prepared the nation for total war—a war that will be won by the nation most capable of mustering the spirit to win, the men to fight, and the resources for combat.

Such movements as Populism, the New Freedom, and the New Deal are but part of a gigantic struggle on the part of common people to make secure life, liberty, and property. While we Americans are prone to think only in terms of our own community and nation, the facts of history reveal that for the past 150 years, especially the past 20 years, mankind has been feverishly searching for security. Fascism, Nazism, Communism, the Popular Front, the New Deal, and scores of other movements are but an indication of a world in transition—a world of the past seeking to adjust itself to the technology of the modern industrial system. Old standards, taboos, customs, and political principles are being destroyed or remodeled. Modern communication and transportation have energized the hopes and aspirations of all men. The poor are more aware of the control and influence of the rich; the rich are fearful of the political power of the poor; the industrialist, protected by a legal code of a laissez faire state, cries out against government regulation. Everywhere change has been evident. New groups seek points of privilege and advantage. Present-day ruling groups or classes sense an atmosphere charged with political and economic revolution.

To those who have studied the rise of parliamentary and democratic institutions this era in which we live should not have been unexpected. A theory of government based on the doctrine of liberty, equality, and fraternity, plus government of the people, by the people, and for the people, is bound to create a desire in the heart of the citizen to secure the blessings of liberty for himself and posterity. The creed of democracy is dynamic; it is contagious; it is expansive. The right to vote, which was but a political promise a century ago, is now a political reality commonly accepted by millions of people in our own nation and others. The democratic citizen of today senses his own importance and his own dignity. Even the so-called illiterate is aware of the potentiality of abundance inherent in the economic resources coupled with modern science. Yes, the citizen of today, be he American, British, French, Italian, German, Chinese, or Japanese, feels that he should share in the fruits of the economy. Whether all people live under republican or democratic institutions is not so important as the fact that the democratic creed has clearly exposed all humanity to the power and wealth inherent in man and the world in which he lives. This does not mean that one should identify the New Deal with Fascism—surely these two programs represent opposites in approach and goals. Although Fascism has sought to subordinate the individual to the rule of the party and the state, boldly denouncing the democratic faith, its rise was due, in a considerable degree, to the political and economic chaos of the postwar period. Surely the general condition of poverty and unemployment did much to facilitate the usurpation of political control by the Fascist clique. Fascism and Nazism found in Italy and Germany a social and political environment conducive to their acceptance. Democratic institutions had failed in both countries, and, in the stress and strain of economic collapse, the leadership principle, with its theory of obedience and subservience to the state, found its way back into the life of the nation. Both Germany and Italy were but a few years removed from the system of monarchy and aristocracy. The same world-wide economic collapse which brought Hitler to power in Germany in 1933, brought Roosevelt and the New Deal to America. These two men today, and the systems they represent, stand locked in mortal combat to test whether "this nation or any nation so conceived and so dedicated can long endure." The America which rested its political ideology on the democratic philosophy of Jefferson, Jackson, Lincoln, Theodore Roosevelt, and Woodrow Wilson waged war on an economic depression by revitalizing democratic instruments rather than goose-stepping in the path of dictatorship. Yet in the month of March, 1933, the positions of Roosevelt and Hitler were strangely similar. Both had risen to power on the crest of a wave of protest against things as they were. Both men and both nations faced problems of unemployment, financial collapse, and the task of inspiring a bewildered and despairing people. We came out with the New Deal and the Germans came out with Nazism because of our heritage of democratic government and because we had chosen as our President the author of the Commonwealth Club speech, while Germany had selected as her chancellor the author of *Mein Kampf* and had a heritage of Wagner, Nietzsche, Prussianism, and Bismarck. Our heritage stood us well. We knew but one answer—one system—that of government by consent and majority rule, government by law and legislature. The crisis proved not to be a catastrophe but a challenge. Americans responded, not by a superstitious veneration of the state, but by reaffirming the traditional view that government is an instrumentality of the people and justified only by the benefits which it confers on the individual men and women who live under it.

The quest for security has become a dynamic movement of such intensity that, in the hope of attaining economic security, one nation after another has sacrificed the principles of political liberty. This we may say is true of the Fascist nations. With the promise of employment, bread, and national prestige millions of people have surrendered their very souls. Apparently not understanding that man is a slave if he relinquishes control over his destiny, the mass of mankind living under Fascism has cast aside political liberty for a mess of pottage. The laboring man in Germany is as much a slave as the American Negro of 1860. If he obeys his master he can live. If he seeks to become his own master, he is exiled or shot.

The counterforce to the Fascist method of integrating twentieth-century technology with an established social system is the democratic procedure. The two systems are in direct opposition. Possibly here is our explanation for the untimely eclipse of recent democratic reform movements. Modern democratic states have all more or less envisioned their security and property as a *national* problem. The international implications of a total world bound together into an economic unit were not realized by democratic statesmen until the enemy was long on the march. The forces of Fascism recognized the economic and political interrelationships of the twentieth-century world. Nazism to be successful, by its own definition of success, must encompass the world. Statesmen of democracy are now just beginning to see that security can be attained for one only if the conditions of security are available to all. Herein lies the challenge to modern democratic principles. There can be no peace, no prosperity, no security in a world forming a total economic unity unless all people in that world become benefactors of the common heritage. The task of democratic statesmanship is not only to evolve programs leading to national security, but to gear their thinking in terms of a world. The original spirit of courage and audacity so clearly evident in the Declaration of Independence must be recaptured—it must be stated in terms that capture the imagination and allegiance of all men. To plan only in terms of helping the "forgotten man" of America is to weaken the possibility of attainment of any social program.

If the New Deal, prior to 1938, has committed any one error of significant importance, it may well be its insistence upon an independent national economic recovery. This policy was, of course, altered by such policies as reciprocal trade treaties and international currency stabilization programs. The Popular Front program of France and the Labor Party program of Britain are guilty of the same thinking and planning. It should be noted, however, that the electorate in all of the democratic countries were fearful of international collaboration. Possibly the blunder of isolationism is testimony to the operation of government by consent of the governed. If such be the case, then history may well record the twentieth century as the era of democracy leading itself to the precipice of disaster.

It is because the author has set himself to a consideration of the New Deal that very little consideration has been given to the foreign policy of the Roosevelt administration. The New Deal is mainly national in its program and concerned primarily with domestic issues. It was developed in the years of comparative peace and in order to be continued it must see the defeat of our enemies.

The Political Philosophy
of the New Deal

CHAPTER 1

Toward an Understanding
of the New Deal

AFTER EIGHT YEARS of New Deal administration there is no unanimity of opinion as to the meaning and objectives of the New Deal. Judged by the strength of the antipathies it has stirred, it is a social movement of revolutionary significance. Judged by the relatively lukewarm quality of the loyalties it has evoked, it would seem to be little more than a collection of palliatives. On June 26, 1936, the day after the Democratic platform was adopted, Mark Sullivan wrote in the New York *Herald Tribune*, "The New Deal is the American variation of the new order that has been set up in three great European countries and some smaller ones. The term 'New Deal' is the American equivalent of the term 'Fascism' in Italy, the term 'Nazi' in Germany, and the term 'Soviet' in Russia." Republican Party leaders have labeled it as a new form of "statism," a semi-dictatorship nourished and perpetuated by generous gifts from the public treasury. Its chief characteristics are an irresponsible bureaucracy, wasteful spending, and crackpot planning. In the view of the Hoover Republicans, the New Deal has not only destroyed free enterprise and regimented industry but has also destroyed the Constitution, defiled the Supreme Court, and demoralized the citizen body. The charges of the opposition are full of "viewing with alarm" and no "pointing with pride." But the quest of the presidency is not conducive to impartial and objective analysis.

While the more conservative of our commentators and politicians have branded the New Deal as un-American and dangerously radical, the so-called leftist has found it to be reactionary and highly capitalistic. It has been described by the Marxist as an outgrowth of the same general economic and social factors which gave rise to Fascism in Germany and Italy. The disintegration of the capitalist economy everywhere menaced the power of monopoly capital. In order to beat back the rising revolt of the working masses and to strengthen their shaken domination, the American capitalist class yielded a few reforms and extended financial aid to the unemployed. This is the sum and substance of the New Deal in the view of the leftist. The evaluation is more Marxist than factual and reveals a failure to understand the circumstances confronting the American people in 1932. The records of the Depression years reveal no mass violence or uprising on the part of the workers; the only display of revolution was to be found among midwestern farmers, organized in the Farmers' Holiday movement.

The New Deal is not without its friends and defenders. Democratic Party leaders have gushed forth a constant stream of oratory "pointing with pride" at the record. It has restored the government to the people, say the New Dealers. It has rescued industry, labor, and the farmer from economic disaster. It has protected the aged, the poor, and the sick; it has stabilized the banks, the insurance companies, and the stock market; it has broken the power of big business and returned the reins of government from Wall Street to Washington, D.C. It has provided for conservation of our national resources; it has doubled the national income. The accomplishments are bounteous; the good performed, inestimable. Yet, in all this amazing record of reform and recovery the politicians have not answered the question, What is the New Deal? What are its purposes, its methods, and its relationship to democratic government? Is it a coherent philosophy, or is it but a mere patchwork of political opportunism? Has it been a force of leadership or has it merely followed? It will be important to determine the effect of the New Deal on such traditions and institutions as individualism, freedom, and private property. Has it altered our constitutional system and if so, what may be the meaning of such changes? It is only with a consideration of these basic questions that we may arrive at some conclusion as to the political philosophy of the New Deal.

President Roosevelt has described the New Deal as a "changed concept of the duty and responsibility of government toward economic life." [1] A. A. Berle, Jr., believes it may be taken as a kind of index for an attitude whose major characteristic is a willingness to accept change and to take political action in terms of that change. The primary objective is to regain economic liberty for the average man.

[1] Franklin D. Roosevelt, *The Public Papers and Addresses* (New York: Random House, 1938), IV, 29.

The method of redemption will be a reordering of the profit system in order to provide economic security without sacrificing political liberty.[2] Ernest K. Lindley has described the New Deal as "democracy trying to create out of American materials an economic system which will work with reasonable satisfaction to the great majority of citizens."[3] It has sought to mend the evils of our condition by reasoned experiment within the framework of the existing social system. If it fails, says John Strachey, "rational change will be gravely prejudiced throughout the world, leaving orthodoxy and revolution to fight it out."[4] Mr. Strachey and a host of other liberal thinkers have sensed the complexity of the problems facing democratic government. The challenge is one of life or death. The issue resolves itself into a question as to the ability of democracy to adjust itself to the problems of industrial capitalism. Where it has failed, Fascism has stepped in to provide order and security. Freedom, as we know it, has been sacrificed for subsistence. The New Deal, faced with an unprecedented economic collapse of the domestic and world economy, chose the course of moderation and rebuilding. It acted boldly to stabilize and to rehabilitate the economic mechanism. It religiously preserved the profit system, even at the price of vast subsidies and direct financial aid to millions of consumers. It was with this thought in mind that

[2] A. A. Berle, Jr., "The New Deal and Economic Liberty," *Annals of the American Academy of Political and Social Sciences,* CLXXVIII (1935), 37–38.

[3] Ernest K. Lindley, *The Roosevelt Revolution* (New York: Viking Press, 1933), 5.

[4] John Strachey, *The Coming Struggle for Power* (New York: The Modern Library, 1935), 397.

Louis M. Hacker described the New Deal as a political program "in behalf of agricultural landlords and big commercial farmers, organized trade unionists, and oversea investors and speculators." [5] For it is these groups that reap the bounteous benefits of the profit system and demand its maintenance.

Partisan loyalty or opposition tends to cloud the objectivity of those who discuss the New Deal. However, one descriptive term seems to have been resorted to by its opponents from the right and even by some of its defenders. Back in 1933, Ernest K. Lindley, of New Deal sympathy, wrote a book which he called *The Roosevelt Revolution.* Former Senator Thomas P. Gore of Oklahoma has said the New Deal was more revolutionary than the Revolution of 1776. H. G. Wells in his book *The New America* stated, "America is undergoing a social if not a political revolution." [6] David Lawrence in a cryptic editorial has analyzed the New Deal, branding it a "revolution of political autocrats," [7] one that spells tyranny and oppression for the individual. This charge, that the New Deal is a revolution, demands that its real nature be subjected to analysis.

A revolution is seldom bloodless or peaceful. It is a device employed by society for the destruction of the constricting molds of class relations; it wipes them out once and for all and changes their solidified forms into a new fluidity. The

[5] Louis M. Hacker, *American Problems of Today* (New York: F. S. Crofts, 1938), 205.

[6] H. G. Wells, *The New America: The New World* (London: The Cressett Press, 1935), 92.

[7] David Lawrence, "The 'Revolution,'" *United States News,* February 16, 1940, pp. 18–19.

history of the more modern revolutionary upheavals is ample proof of this conclusion. As long as an economic society is in its youth and the economy is an expanding one, revolution is unusual and improbable. But as an economic society grows into maturity and old age, the class lines harden and class relationships get out of balance. The leading problem shifts from expansion into new fields, to consolidation of those already won. Then oppression becomes the unconcealed weapon of the ruling group and class hostilities become open. The result of the continued oppression is revolution and the emergence of a new ruling group. Class lines again become flexible and the economy becomes readjusted to the pattern of the new leading group.[8] Obviously, in terms of these considerations, the New Deal is not a revolution. Its rationale may be stated in the following propositions. The New Deal recognized that the American economy had changed from one of expansion to one of intensive consolidation. It had slowed down and the forces within the economy were out of balance.[9] Opportunities for capitalist enterprise had contracted. The population had ceased expanding; there were few, if any, new great industrial fields to be opened up; and foreign trade had been seriously injured by cutthroat competition and high tariff barriers. Capitalism was actually confronted by a sharp decrease in the rate of profit and the security of investment. The New Dealer noticed that control had shifted from industrial capitalism to finance capi-

---

[8] Louis M. Hacker, *A Short History of the New Deal* (New York: F. S. Crofts, 1934), 24–27.

[9] See Richard V. Gilbert and others, *An Economic Program for American Democracy* (New York: The Vanguard Press, 1938).

talism. The objective of business was no longer the seeking of legitimate economic expansion; instead, emphasis was laid on the exploitation of investors and the consuming public by stock market manipulation and monopoly price maintenance. It was evident that the spread between capacity to produce and ability to consume had constantly widened; imperialism revealed its inability to provide all the needed outlets for surplus capital. The world market for agricultural products had largely disappeared and a decline in farm values had set in. By 1932 it had become evident that opportunities for new jobs were few. The labor market had an oversupply of workers, and capital could find no willing investors. Agriculture had become burdened with an unbearable indebtedness, and the wholesale foreclosure on farm properties threatened the safety of orderly government. The domestic market was unable to consume farm produce, and the feeble attempts to control crop surpluses by the Federal Farm Board proved a failure. Class lines were being clearly drawn; the danger of class hostilities was no longer remote but already in evidence. Then, too, under the operation of the so-called capitalistic free market the owners or the controllers of the means of production, because of their greater strength, size, and organization, could continue to maintain themselves perhaps for a long time; but their security would depend upon the steady debasement of the standards of living of the other classes of society.[10]

The seeds of revolution or counterrevolution were present in such a situation. The hardening of class lines and the

[10] Hacker, *A Short History of the New Deal*, 26.

entrenchment of organized wealth at the expense of labor, farmer, and small business would eventually lead to the creation of conditions favorable to violent reaction. The philosophers of the New Deal had no desire to see the revolution. They refused to lose faith in the capitalistic system. Their creed called for positive action to save private enterprise and to set the system in balance. The New Dealers have had no intention of overhauling drastically the capitalist system. They felt the mechanism had run down temporarily and the solution was to wind it up again, after certain repairs have been made and new parts substituted.[11] There has been no concerted attack on private enterprise. Private ownership of the means of production is to continue. The aim has been to prevent capitalism from exploiting both its labor supply and the producers of raw material. The wage earner has been given basic guarantees in the form of minimum wages and social security. While the hope has been that a higher standard of living may be achieved, subsistence has been assured. President Roosevelt has stated the position of the New Deal in its relationship to capitalism:

No one in the United States believes more firmly than I in the system of private business, private property, and private profit. . . . If the Administration had had the slightest inclination to change that system, all that it would have had to do was to fold its hands and wait—let the system continue to default to itself and to the public. Instead we did what the previous administration had declined to do through all the years of the

---

[11] See Hacker, *A Short History of the New Deal*; Hacker, *American Problems of Today*; Strachey, *The Coming Struggle for Power*; and Ernest K. Lindley, *Half Way with Roosevelt* (New York: Viking Press, 1936).

depression. We acted quickly and drastically to save it. It was because of our belief in private enterprise that we acted quickly and drastically to save it. It was because of our belief in private enterprise that we acted, because of our faith in the essential and fundamental virtue of democracy and our conviction that individual initiative and private profit served it best.[12]

The New Deal has sought to establish a balance between American class relations. Far from desiring to enthrone the proletariat in any of its measures, it would seem to me the real objective is to abolish the proletariat, or rather make it wholly unnecessary by lifting it into a different state. Instead of endeavoring to create an equalitarianism, it has endeavored to liberate inequalities or to permit a more just recognition of inequalities. In that desire, instead of following the totalitarian doctrines proposed by the Communists, it has taken an individualistic attack, endeavoring to make something available to the individual so that thereafter he can take care of himself.[13] The idea of establishing a balance between American class relations occurs again and again in the writings and speeches of President Roosevelt and his advisers. It has been assumed that it is possible to establish a permanent truce on class antagonisms. The devices the New Deal has mainly relied on are the restoration of the purchasing power and a more equitable distribution of national income. Roosevelt has expressed the principle clearly: "What we seek is balance in our economic system—balance between agriculture and industry and balance between the wage-earner, the employer and

[12] Franklin D. Roosevelt, speech of October 23, 1936, in *The Public Papers and Addresses*, V, 534.

[13] Berle, "The New Deal and Economic Liberty," 45–46.

the consumer."[14] To the New Dealer good government should maintain the balance where every individual may find safety if he wishes it, where every individual may attain such power as his ability permits.[15]

The readjustments cannot be termed revolution in the historical meaning of the term, but implicit in all of this is a call for a changed conception of economy and life. For more than a hundred years the American economy has been essentially speculative and a dominant national ideal has been that of getting rich as quickly as possible. Even agriculture has been a huge venture in land speculation rather than a way of life. The stock market has been a kind of national shrine. The national objective has been to open up and develop this great country, regardless of waste or expense. The New Deal has sought to change this national ideal. It has insisted upon stabilization, steady price levels, and reasonable security for all. It has sought to equalize privilege by the helping hand of government. It has desired to bring about governmental action to mesh more with the rights and essential needs of the individual. It seeks to preserve the capitalistic system, but the operations of that system are to be hedged in the interests of the security of the workingman, the farmer, and the small investor. It has no desire to destroy individual liberty, but rather seeks to adjust personal freedom with the social good. If in these things clear-cut novelty is not discernible, there is in them a sharpness and weight of emphasis sufficient to make the New Deal signalize a break with much

[14] Franklin D. Roosevelt, *The Public Papers and Addresses*, III, 232.
[15] Franklin D. Roosevelt, *Looking Forward* (New York: John Day Co., 1933), 9–10.

of our historic past. There can be no doubt but that the activities of the Roosevelt administration are so completely directed to the attainment of social rather than individual ends that to many, who had been brought up on the automatic operations of the laissez faire economy, a veritable revolution threatened.[16]

Much confusion as to the policies of the New Deal has arisen because of the method of approach to the problems it seeks to solve. Most of us are essentially doctrinaire and dogmatic in our economic and political beliefs. We have been schooled in the eternal verity of the law of supply and demand and the perfectibility of democratic institutions. We are more faithful than inquisitive, more conservative than courageous. Against the essential conservatism of a highly developed business economy, the New Deal attacked the problems of the social and economic maladjustment with a trial-and-error method. This philosophy has been termed pragmatism or experimentalism. The main characteristic of the pragmatist is action. Act, even if you act mistakenly. Pragmatism is a combination of thinking and doing. Professor John Dewey, the greatest exponent of pragmatic philosophy, has said that

... the best test of consequences is more exacting than that afforded by fixed general rules. When new acts are tried, new results are experienced, while the lauded immutability of eternal ideas and forms is in itself a denial of the possibility of development and improvement. . . . Ideals serve vaguely to arouse aspirations, but they do not evoke any direct strivings for embodiment in actual existence. . . . Progress is more sound when laws, principles, standards, and ideals are not regarded as

---

[16] Hacker, *A Short History of the New Deal*, 15–20.

something to swear by and stick to at all hazards, but when clews and tests found within concrete acts are employed instead. . . . In principle, experimental method does not signify random and aimless action—it implies direction by ideas and knowledge.[17]

What does all this mean, in simpler language? It means that the pragmatic experimental philosophy calls for being bold, and, if necessary, somewhat revolutionary in order to attain better results. It is not afraid of the new. Neither does it cling to the old. It is adventurous, willing to take risks. It is scientific in temper, everlastingly desirous of going forward and of doing something about an unsatisfactory situation, even if one experiment must be abandoned and a new one tried.[18]

It has only to be explained in this way to see that the Roosevelt and New Deal philosophy tends toward the pragmatic, experimental, and objective. It is, therefore, more directly scientific; and it explains why Roosevelt likes and uses his "Brain Trust," whereas Woodrow Wilson, a much more subjective, idealistic person, could not have used such a plan or held such a philosophy. Also, it reveals how Herbert Hoover, full of "set" ideas of what "must not be done" and what "cannot be done," was unable to meet the problems which beset his administration. He had many fixed ideas which he refused to alter when new conditions arose, and he shrank from bold experiment. Splendid man though he was, the fast pace of the times outraced him.

[17] John Dewey, *The Quest for Certainty: A Study of the Relation of Knowledge and Action* (New York: Minton, Balch & Co., 1929), 77.
[18] J. George Frederick, *A Primer of New Deal Economics* (New York: The Business Bourse, 1933), 154.

"The day for pragmatic action had come; swiftness of economic change forced it." [19]

Mr. Roosevelt has the type of mind to which little is impossible and nothing inevitable. Blind faith in the self-restorative powers of capitalism, the certainty of its doom— both are alien to his way of thinking. He has never been a doctrinaire. Reared in the self-confident tradition, his observations of the world have never driven him to refuge in a creed. With a sense of continual movement that comes from the study of history and practical experience in politics, Mr. Roosevelt is fully aware that the "iron laws" of successive schools of orthodox economists, no less than the patent remedies of successive schools of visionaries, have been ground to bits by the interplay of changing forces.[20] Thus, in attacking the Depression, the New Deal has not acted bound by any creed or "party line," but has, in part, adopted the trial-and-error method. The Chief Executive openly admits that he does not know the solution to every economic and social issue confronting his administration. He demanded "bold, persistent experimentation" a year before his inauguration, and he has said repeatedly that his method is to try something and if that fails to try something else. His speech at Oglethorpe University in May, 1932, reveals his position in no uncertain words: "True leadership calls for the setting forth of objectives and the rallying of public opinion in support of these objectives. . . . The country needs, and, unless I mistake its temper, the country demands bold, persistent experimentation. It is

[19] *Ibid.*, 156.
[20] Lindley, *The Roosevelt Revolution*, 15.

common sense to take a method and try it; if it fails, admit it frankly and try another. But above all, try something." [21] This experimental attitude forbids adherence to any hard and fast program. It does, or did in the case of Mr. Roosevelt, suppose an objective. It is important to note that Mr. Roosevelt advocated experimental tactics, not for the mere pleasure of experimentation, but as a means for climbing out of the Depression and also for achieving a better and more stable economic order that would assure the greatest happiness to the greatest number.

It is said that President Roosevelt has used a football game analogy to explain his mode of action. He is the quarterback. He knows where the goal line is. At any given moment he can call the signal for the next play, but he cannot decide what the play after the next will be until he has seen whether the first play has resulted in a gain or loss.[22] This is the experimental method in action. It is a complete repudiation of the doctrinaire faith that every play will work with mechanical precision and unfailing success. It recognizes also that every play, every motion, must be executed by men, so that even the most perfectly conceived attack may bog down and fail through imperfect performance. It also implies that the quarterback may err in his judgment.

It should be clearly understood that the New Deal is not fully pragmatic. It leans toward it, not wholeheartedly accepting it. By its rigid adherence to democratic processes and to the essential features of the capitalistic econ-

---

[21] Franklin D. Roosevelt, address at Oglethorpe University, May 22, 1932, in *The Public Papers and Addresses,* I, 646.

[22] Frederick, *A Primer of New Deal Economics,* 151–68.

omy, it repudiates the complete objectivity of scientific method. It is pragmatic only so far as the flexibility of the Constitution and the system of private enterprise permit. The acceptance of pragmatic experimentalism is not an end in itself, but a means toward rehabilitating democratic government and capitalism. The objective of the New Deal, "the greatest good for the greatest number," is to be attained through a definite accepted social and political system. The pragmatism of the New Deal stops at the gateway of immediate fundamental change in either the political or economic order. Thus, the New Deal is neither revolution nor counterrevolution. It is neither 100 percent pragmatic nor 100 percent doctrinaire. It is American democracy working within the political and economic limitations of established government and private enterprise.

CHAPTER 2

One from Many

THE DEPRESSION was in the middle of its third year when the presidential contest of 1932 gained momentum. The Republican Party had faithfully renominated President Hoover in a rather unspectacular convention. The platform was a conservative document, considering the gravity of the situation. It pledged the continuance of the gold standard; voiced its love for American industry, labor, and the farmer; was indefinite on the prohibition issue; promised veterans benefits; defended the Hawley-Smoot Tariff Act of 1930; and pledged the party to world peace.[1]

The Democratic Party nominated Franklin D. Roosevelt as its standard-bearer. The platform was a model of conciseness but one "under whose flag almost any Democrat could have sailed." [2] To this platform the candidate pledged himself 100 percent, flying from Albany, New York, to

[1] Hacker, *A Short History of the New Deal,* 13–14.
[2] *Ibid.,* 15.

deliver his acceptance message in person, thereby abolishing a time-worn custom of formal notification and a belated acceptance of the honor.

Franklin D. Roosevelt had been a successful but not a great governor. No doubt he had been extremely careful of his every action in order not to injure his chances as a preconvention candidate. However, a careful reading of his numerous preconvention speeches will reveal in broad outlines the entire New Deal program and objectives. Of course, circumstances and changing conditions have altered the details but the main tenets of the New Deal philosophy are clearly evident.

The presidential campaign in the summer and fall of 1932 found Roosevelt vigorously challenging the Republican leadership and discussing with considerable skill the problems of the Depression and the way out. One obvious distinction between the positions of the two candidates began to emerge as the campaign progressed. Mr. Hoover attributed the Depression to international causes; Mr. Roosevelt boldly asserted that most of the nation's difficulties were domestic in origin. Ernest K. Lindley sums up the matter: "The program of the New Deal, as originally conceived, as developed in Mr. Roosevelt's speeches . . . was essentially national. It was predicated on the feasibility of independent economic recovery by the United States, and its long-range objective was the reshaping of the American economic system." [3] While Mr. Roosevelt, in the early days of the New Deal, expressed belief in the domestic origins of the Depression, his attitude did not express the

[3] Lindley, *The Roosevelt Revolution*, 112.

sum total opinion of the New Deal. Tempered by the advice and experience of Cordell Hull, plus that of the New Deal economists, his administration soon recognized the international implications.

As the campaign gained momentum, it became evident that the Republican leadership would be defeated. That much was certain by October, 1932. The question that perplexed the political commentator was "this man Roosevelt." He had been generally regarded as an affable and charming gentleman who spoke well and was a master of the arts of conciliation and compromise, but he occasionally made public utterances which seemed to upset the decorum of high finance and gentlemanly society. A close reading of his early addresses, both as governor and presidential candidate, will show, however, that he was not hostile to private enterprise or the capitalistic system and, therefore, in the final analysis, that he is no radical; but the operations of the system were to be hedged around so closely in the interests of the security of the workingman, farmer, and small investor, and its activities were to be directed so completely to the attainment of social rather than individual ends that to many, who had been brought up on the automatic operations of the laissez faire economy, a veritable revolution threatened. To the great mass of the American people he appeared as the man of the hour, the man who could lead the nation back to prosperity. The results of the election were indicative of the desire by the people for a new attitude on the part of government. The Republican leadership was swept from office, and the Democratic Party regained the presidency after twelve long years of waiting. The way was now clear for the inauguration of the New Deal—the descriptive phrase which had come to be associated with the policies that Roosevelt and his advisers had so hopefully outlined.

Doctrinaires have had an especially difficult time in understanding the New Deal, and their efforts to explain it have usually added to the general confusion. The New Deal is not a "doctrine, nor a system, but the result of a mingling of doctrines, ideas, influences, political groups and pressures." [4] It should be made clear that a great many people had a share in the creation of the New Deal, including the public itself. A great leader's policies are always molded and altered by those who raise him to leadership, and Franklin D. Roosevelt is no exception. His ability is expressed quite particularly in his capacity to coordinate the thought of competent advisers and to interpret public opinion. The New Deal must, therefore, be considered as a composite of many minds in many political camps and occupations. The President and his Cabinet received thousands of "plans" which are significant of the enormous activity of American minds in endeavoring to shape the new program.

It must be conceded that Roosevelt was elected not so much for his program but more as a protest of discontented groups against the Republican leadership. The political atmosphere of early 1933 was charged with an earnest desire for change—change in party and some sort of change in our economic system. It is true that the average person did not know exactly what should be done, but there was present in America an emotional distrust of things as they

[4] Lindley, *Half Way with Roosevelt*, 36.

were. It was a kind of "fed-up" feeling. Sometimes the desire for change took the simple form of prejudice against those in power; then again it tended toward a complete reorganization of our economic system.[5]

Coupled with an intuitive desire for a change there was an awakening desire for more idealism in our economic life. The Depression had stopped a materialistic orgy. It also started fermenting a sense of guilt and shame for the excesses of speculation, materialism, and business ethics. The shock of being parted so suddenly from material possessions and of having smug notions of economics overturned was so great that people's minds were seeking new and other values. The terrifying spectacle of riot and hunger in a land of abundance challenged the heart and mind of the most hardheaded. The sense of emptiness that came with the collapse of business values stimulated a spiritual or idealistic awakening that demanded recognition in social and economic planning. Nothing was more logical than the development of some sort of "New Deal" economics, set in a framework of a new idealism, "a reorientation of economic purpose on a broader and less selfish basis, for really universal not merely individualistic welfare." [6]

Motivated by earnest desire for change and the demand for a new idealism, powerful organized political and pressure groups advanced innumerable panaceas and guaranteed cures for the domestic troubles. It seems to be axiomatic that the more serious the trouble, the more confident the prescriber. A shorter work week with increased pay, infla-

---

[5] Frederick, *A Primer of New Deal Economics*, 27–30.
[6] *Ibid.*, 30.

tion, technocracy, pensions, doles, production-for-use, and state ownership were recommended. Every remedy was guaranteed by its proponent, and anyone who might distrust its feasibility was branded a radical or a reactionary. Lashed by the waves of these simple but sure-cure economic and political pressures, the New Deal attempted to steer a middle course, hoping to satisfy a majority, and yet to continue to function within democratic principles and a capitalistic economy.

One of the powerful influences seeking recognition was the deflationist group, which may be termed the laissez faire or natural recovery school. Its theory, supported by observation of the past, is that capitalism contains self-correcting forces which guarantee that if everybody sits tight and will wait long enough, a depression will end automatically and another period of prosperity will follow. The adoption of the deflationist method would have involved wholesale liquidation and complete collapse of the American economic structure. The adherents of this theory ignored the changes that had taken place in business. No longer was the economy a decentralized system of small-business units. The growth of corporations and finance capitalism had molded widespread activity of a great nation into a delicate mechanism, the operation of which was supersensitive to any maladjustment. No doubt, the deflationist advocates had orthodox Adam Smith economics on their side. Capitalism does necessitate a certain amount of housecleaning every so often. However, the difference between housecleaning and housewrecking was not recognized by this group. To have permitted the continuance of wholesale mortgage foreclosures, business failures, and bank crashes would not have merely squeezed out the sub-marginal producer or operator but would have engulfed the entire financial structure. Insurance companies depended on railroad and industrial stability; industry depended on banks; banks depended on insurance; and so on. These factors the New Deal economists and leaders recognized, and, although it was necessary to permit a reasonable amount of liquidation, the flow of losses had to be checked before all was lost. It may be that the New Deal program attempted to save a "dead horse" or it may have been too softhearted to allow the necessary economic bloodletting. Be that as it may, it did not allow deflation to run its course. Capitalism had developed to a point where financial liquidation, unimpeded, meant the end of capitalism. The state, long considered the enemy of free enterprise, became the savior. Controls over the economic life of the nation had developed the twofold purpose of being able to liquidate and then check liquidation; of being able to regulate, yet not regiment.

Closely allied to the deflationist school are those who saw the cure for our economic ills in the restoration of international trade.[7] Here was the old Democratic Party economics asserting its influence. The exponents of international free trade were intent upon removing such obstacles as tariffs, unstable currencies, exchange controls, quotas, and embargoes. This particular influence found its partial realization in the New Deal reciprocal trade agreements program. While tariffs and exchange controls have not been abolished, the principle of reciprocity has aimed

[7] Lindley, *Half Way with Roosevelt*, 37.

at easing the restriction on the flow of goods and through careful adjustment of tariff schedules produced some semblance of sanity in American trade policies. It is a far cry from "free trade" and at best a compromise plan between high-protection pressures at home and economic readjustment abroad. The pressure of the old Democratic Party economics, represented by the illustrious Cordell Hull, did much to alter the essential nationalistic interpretation of the Depression, its causes and cures.

In a third group, which, though small in the administration inner circles, is large in Congress and supported by powerful agrarian pressure, may be placed the currency manipulators—the inflationists.[8] This group's influence was reflected in the theory that recovery will come primarily from reduction of the gold content of the dollar (or from that plus the silver purchasing program) and that nothing more needs to be done. It received its recognition in the Thomas Amendment to the Agricultural Adjustment Act, providing authority for the President to issue some three billion dollars in greenbacks, and in the gold-purchasing and price-fixing program. The debtor group in the American economy has traditionally supported the inflationist or currency expansion scheme. In times of severe depression the influence of this common man's panacea always finds its way into the congressional policies. From Shays's Rebellion to Jackson's wildcat banks, to Lincoln's greenbacks, through Bryan's Cross of Gold speech, the voice of a debtor class has sought relief in currency expansion and the abolition of the gold standard.

[8] *Ibid.*, 39–40.

The inflationist idea merges into a fourth view: that, with monetary management combined with suitable taxation, subsidies, and other "compensatory" measures, the capitalistic system can be made to operate with reasonable success and stability. This particular viewpoint is held by many of the administration leaders and is often referred to as "pump-priming." It involves considerable financial regulations—for example, over banks, industry, and agriculture. It is perhaps best represented by Marriner S. Eccles, chairman of the board of governors of the Federal Reserve System.[9]

A fifth group, very prominent in early New Deal activities, consisted of organized labor.[10] The powerful support given Mr. Roosevelt in the 1934 and 1936 elections by organized labor placed this group in a position where its voice could not be ignored. The demands of labor centered around higher wages, shorter hours, legalization and protection of collective bargaining rights, and a few other well defined and familiar devices. Section 7(a) of the National Industrial Recovery Act signifies labor's strength in the first days of the New Deal, and, with recovery in industry, the administration sponsored the National Labor Relations Act, the Wages and Hours Act, and numerous other enactments for the benefit of labor. The more aggressive wing of organized labor merges into the group represented by Secretary of Labor Frances Perkins and Senator Robert F. Wagner of New York, who have led the fight for unemployment insurance, old age insurance,

[9] *Ibid.,* 39. Also see Gilbert and others, *An Economic Program for American Democracy.*
[10] *Ibid.,* 40.

and other forms of social insurance, as well as slum clearance, housing projects, and other measures for increasing the security and improving the working and living conditions of wage earners.

A seventh group may be designated as the old-fashioned progressives.[11] The nightmare of these valiant soldiers of democracy is "big business" and its cohort "Wall Street." They would reform the practices and reduce the power of high finance and reverse the collectivist trend embodied in the growth of large corporations and holding companies. They seek to decentralize industry, encourage small business, and crush monopoly. The strength of this school is bolstered by a long and painful experience with predatory financiers and lesser manipulators and is rooted in the belief that the polarization of wealth and the centralization of power over wealth are incompatible with the continued existence of a democratic society. It should be remembered that this is one of the mainstreams of thought flowing into the New Deal. It found its voice on the Supreme Court in Justice Brandeis and is a powerful factor in Congress, especially among the midwestern representatives.

Closely akin to the old-fashioned progressivist school of thought is the influence of the conservationist. No one more clearly represents this group than the Chief Executive himself. His policies both as governor of the state of New York and as President have been directed toward a grandiose plan of conservation of natural resources and human life. The Civilian Conservation Corps, the reforestation service, the soil conservation program, soil erosion program,

[11] Lindley, *Half Way with Roosevelt*, 39.

flood control, and irrigation projects are all part of a great national plan to conserve our natural resources. The Chief Executive has been able to direct the activities of the Work Projects Administration, the Tennessee Valley Authority, the Boulder Dam project, and numerous other agencies and services into a concerted attack on conservation problems. It is, without a doubt, one of the main tenets of the New Deal program. The truth of this evaluation can best be attested to by these words of the President:

Men and nature must work hand in hand. The throwing off balance of the resources of nature throws out of balance also the lives of men. . . . We think of our land and water and human resources not as static and sterile possessions, but as life giving assets to be directed by wise provision for future days. We seek to use our natural resources not as a thing apart but as something that is interwoven with industry, labor, finance, taxation, agriculture, homes, recreation, and good citizenship. The results of this interweaving will have a greater influence on the future American standard of living than all the rest of our economics put together.[12]

It is evident that Mr. Roosevelt's conservation program includes much more than mere forest, mine, and water conservation. It embraces the entire national economy and opens the way to hitherto undreamed-of measures of public planning and control.

In an eighth group that helped to elect the New Deal ticket might be placed the "export crop" farmers and the farm organization leaders who had been fighting, for a decade before Mr. Roosevelt's nomination, for parity with industry. It had sponsored the ill-fated McNary-Haugen

[12] Franklin D. Roosevelt, *The Public Addresses and Papers*, IV, 59–60.

bills during Republican days and had been demanding agricultural aid with increasing pressure on Congress. This group represented not only the demand of certain types of farmers for more income, loans, and subsidies, but to some extent held that "if agricultural income were kept up, the American economic system would run fairly well without much other tinkering." The efforts of the New Deal administration in the form of crop control, subsidies, marketing control, and other devices embodied in farm relief legislation are indicative of the power of this group.[13]

Any attempt to study the New Deal by an analysis of the groups or pressures embodied within its framework would be wholly incomplete without a consideration of that much-heralded and criticized group known as the "Brain Trust." It must be obvious to anyone that, even in normal times, a President of the United States is confronted with more problems of consequence than he can fully inform himself about. Under the conditions of a "silent revolution" and a grave panic crisis, this situation is multiplied many times. No one man could be wise and able enough to see through to sound solution of all the new problems of a great period of social and economic change.

The truth is that the Brain Trust has no reality except as a loose, unorganized, and unofficial set of researchers and advisers, separate from the Cabinet, who are used by the President to formulate clear and well-integrated policies.

[13] "To date the federal treasury has spent more than $3,000,000,000 to support the farm program, which is now costing more than a billion a year." "Socialized Agriculture," *United States News*, March 22, 1940, p. 29.

The Brain Trust's place in the New Deal is primarily that of a research and consultation department in a large corporation. It deals with fundamental principles and seeks to cordinate a program. Although the personnel of this inner circle has changed, the general purpose has remained steadfast. It seeks to act in an advisory capacity and to formulate programs. The President has sensed the need of experts and farseeing men. It is to be noted that he has faith primarily in hammering out ideas in personal conference and discussion among a few highly competent minds, rather than in long commission reports or one-man advice. Thus, the so-called Brain Trust may be said to be a kind of private smithy "for heating, treating, pounding, and welding ideas which are to be presented as the Presidents' own, or as New Deal principles." [14]

The New Deal has placed considerable responsibility and faith in this trained personnel. The Chief Executive and his department heads have relied on experts to an unprecedented extent in the formulation of legislation and policy. The words of Mr. Harold L. Ickes, secretary of the interior, present the administration's attitude toward planning and experts: "As the welfare of the people becomes more and more dependent upon the proper working of government, as it undeniably does as our economic system becomes more and more involved, it becomes increasingly important for the government to have in its service the best talent available and to contrive with that talent for the best use of the country's resources. The best use must always have as its aim the greatest good of the greatest

[14] Frederick, *A Primer of New Deal Economics*, 80.

number of citizens." [15] It should be noted that the Brain Trusters have been more than a little responsible for much of the social legislation of the New Deal and that by their research and studied suggestions Mr. Roosevelt has been able to coordinate many special and separate activities into a more or less unified program of social action. The President and his Brain Trusters have made the New Deal "a curious combination of humanitarian reform and practical social idealism." [16]

Not only can we discover numerous and diverse economic groups assembled under the banner of the New Deal —all seeking to promote their own special interests and all ready, willing, and able to dispense their own perfected cure for our economic troubles—but we are able to classify these several groups into four categories of so-called liberalism. First we have the Adam Smith economic liberal, or the laissez faire exponent. He believes in the free market-place, in the automatic economic system, one which is healthy and sound only when left alone. In practice, throughout the past 150 years, this theory has been repeatedly set aside under the pressure of practical necessity. These same exponents of nineteenth-century liberalism have repeatedly called on government to help business in countless ways, from the protective tariff to dollar diplomacy and the Reconstruction Finance Corporation.[17]

The recent report of the Temporary National Economic

[15] Harold L. Ickes, *The New Democracy* (New York: W. W. Norton & Co., Inc., 1934), 154.

[16] Alfred M. Bingham, "The New Deal Has a Future," *Common Sense*, August, 1939, p. 8.

[17] David Cushman Coyle, "The American Way," *Harper's Monthly Magazine*, February, 1938, p. 229.

Committee (T.N.E.C.) pays service to this ideal. Sharply criticizing numerous financial and industrial policies of the New Deal and reiterating the "curse of bigness" in monopoly, industry, and finance, the committee calls for decentralization of capital and industry. It fervently advocates renewed application of antitrust legislation. Competition must be maintained or regained. The menace of concentrated economic power challenges the existence of free enterprise and political democracy.

There is a second kind of liberal—the small-enterprise liberal. He has abandoned all notions of an automatic system, or even the notion of one regulated through the common-law courts.[18] He recognizes the monstrous fact of the concentration of economic power. But in his plans for vanquishing that power, he rejects the premise of the new collectivism that large-scale industry is inevitable and the problem now is for the state to control or operate it. This typically American small businessman wants competition enforced and is willing to have the state act affirmatively in economic terms to get it enforced. He wants enterprise broken up into smaller units and depends on the government to do it. His hope lies in the antitrust laws and their vigorous enforcement. This type of liberal has seen his best days, but continues to look to the Roosevelt administration for the accomplishment of the all important task of "trust-busting."

The New Deal has brought forth another unique species of liberal, all its own—the administrative liberal. He differs

[18] Max Lerner, *It Is Later Than You Think* (New York: Viking Press, 1939), 19.

from the small-enterprise liberal not only in his tendencies toward socialization of the huge economic aggregates, but also in the "astringent mood with which he confronts the claims of the financial community to decisive power in industry or government." [19] The administrative liberal has an acute sensitiveness toward any attempt to sabotage government control and possesses a sense of urgency for making government power equal to its tasks. His emphasis is concentrated throughout upon the effectiveness of the administrative process and the executive power. He, too, is a capitalist and desires to see the system perpetuated, but under adequate social controls. For him, labor gains, such as collective bargaining and unionism, are not ends in themselves but means for stabilizing and tempering capitalism. He wants to make capitalism function in order to avert a violent revolution, but he is not content to scrap the claims of social justice in the process. The Brain Trust group is the chief exponent of this philosophy, while such senators as Wagner of New York and Claude Pepper of Florida, along with former Congressman Maury Maverick of Texas, may be included. I would say that any one attitude typifying the New Deal philosophy would be that of the administrative liberal.

There is a fourth and new type of liberal emerging—the democratic collectivist. The rise of organized labor's power has given impetus to this new progressive politician. His leanings are to the left, toward a program of democratic socialization. He is, like the administrative liberal, a gradualist, but is not so prone to compromise and temporize.

---

[19] *Ibid.*, 20.

"He regards unionism not only as a method for better circulation of purchasing power but as a new cultural base for democracy."[20] This liberal force has found its chief political power in certain sections of the C.I.O. The most casual observer has sensed the political pressure of this group, and the New Deal administration has met its demands on numerous occasions.

The writer has attempted in the short space of a few pages to present some of the main ideas, influences, creeds, and pressures in the New Deal. The list could be expanded and broken down into subdivisions until it reached its end in a catalog of individuals. The purpose of this cross-section study has been to expose to the reader some of the factors and forces that must be taken into consideration by the President and his administration in the formulation of a program. Any modern party, if it hopes to succeed and stay in power, must be able to satisfy the demands of the electorate and more particularly its supporters. The New Deal is more than the old Democratic Party—it is the old party plus all of those groups and interests that were and are distrustful and disgusted with the Republican Party and its leadership. To be able to produce a program that has any semblance of consistency or unified purpose, and at the same time satisfy dozens of diverse sectional and economic groups, has been a herculean task. It is with this in mind that we must judge the New Deal.

A prominent critic of Franklin Roosevelt has written, "I do not blame Mr. Roosevelt unduly for inconsistency. . . . A politician who maintains a complete consistency all

[20] *Ibid.*, 21.

of his life assumes his own infallibility and will destroy his country if he stays in power." [21] To be able to determine the consistency or inconsistency of any program or programs we must first decide whether we mean *ends* or *means*. That is, if we are to expect that every action, let us say, every bit of legislation, shall be carried out in the same manner and for the same people, then no one can claim that the New Deal has claim to any semblance of consistency. But, if we set as the criterion the objective or the end of all administrative and legislative acts, then the New Deal, because of its professed objective that "every government policy should first be laid against the specification of the greatest good for the greatest number of individual men and women," [22] may lay claim to a consistent policy.

It is not the purpose of the writer to give any detailed discussion of the New Deal activities and the numerous agencies set up to carry out the enacted policies. The scope and magnitude of the recovery measures and the pump-priming activities have been commonplace knowledge. This much, however, should be noted: the New Deal, in its attempt to halt the Depression and restore prosperity, has not overlooked any section or group in the American nation. True, it has given much more assistance to organized labor than it has to unorganized labor; it has materially aided the commercial farmer while doing comparatively little for the tenant and submarginal producer. It has lent the financial support of the government to big business,

[21] Charles P. Taft, *You and I and Roosevelt* (New York: Farrar and Rinehart, Inc., 1936), 26.
[22] Franklin D. Roosevelt, *Looking Forward*, 193.

while doing little or nothing in the form of loans and credits for small business.[23] All of this is true in part, but it is not a valid criticism of the New Deal in that it fails to recognize the avowed purpose of the program—the greatest good for the greatest number. The President, whom we must identify as synonymous with the New Deal, and his advisers have felt that the best manner in which to help everyone was to stabilize the forces of industrial production and agricultural producers and to guarantee certain rights to labor. In other words, the first aim in the entire New Deal program has been to check the disastrous downward spiral of economic depression. This has been attempted by a twofold attack: one plan has been to render substantial financial aid to American business, while at the same time putting a stop to the excesses and abuses that had grown up in corporate enterprise; the second has been to assure the necessities of life through financial aid to those who were unable to provide for themselves, which aid would in turn be spent in the channels of trade and thereby revive the economic system and furnish employment for the jobless. No doubt, the New Deal has offered its major assistance to the owners of property and to corporate business. This was felt to be necessary due to the magnitude and importance of big business in our economic system. However, in rendering such aid, the New Deal has attempted to see to it that the same abuses which caused the Depression do not continue to exist. In this manner, it has hoped to revitalize and reorganize the eco-

[23] Hacker, *American Problems of Today*, 200.

nomic life of the nation so as to make a place for everyone who is willing and able to work.

In a recent book by Louis M. Hacker, we find the following evaluation and criticism of the New Deal:

The New Deal, to put it boldly, assumed that it was possible to establish a permanent truce on class antagonisms. The private ownership of the means of production was to continue; but capitalism was to be stopped from exploiting, on the one hand, the producers of raw materials, and, on the other hand, its labor supply. Agriculture, despite its over-capitalized plant and its growing restriction to the labor market, was to get a large enough return to allow for the meeting of fixed charges and the purchase of capital and consumer goods. Wage earners were to be assured employment and at least means of subsistence, if not incomes conducive to a decent standard of living. This idea of establishing a balance between American class relations occurred frequently in the writings and utterances of Mr. Roosevelt and his advisors.[24]

It should be added to Mr. Hacker's conclusions that, while the New Deal has concentrated its major expenditures and energies for the benefit of the landowner, corporate business, organized labor, and the capitalist in general, it has (by its experiments in slum clearance, in public health, in farm rehabilitation or farm resettlement programs, and in regional planning such as the Tennessee Valley Authority) set in motion ideas of social pioneering that fundamentally challenge the old order of things. The democratic state of laissez faire vintage has manifested tendencies of the social democratic state—the service state. The underprivileged member of society is to be cared for not only because of

[24] *Ibid.,* 199.

humanitarian sympathy but because the economic system can ill afford to allow a great proportion of its clientele to become poverty-stricken and restless. To be sure, the New Deal has expended its major energies on the more productive segments of the economy, but behind this rather temporary rejuvenation lies the long-range plan of rehabilitating millions of underprivileged and dispossessed consumers and producers. This process of rehabilitation is to be performed within the confines of democratic political principles and private enterprise. The power of government is exerted only to stimulate the recovery and assure the permanency of the cure.

This is no mere personal design on the part of Roosevelt and his advisers. The evolutionary development of an economic system from the hand plow and the frontier to the mass-production factory and finance capitalism brought in its progression ever-increasing social and economic maladjustment. A preponderant majority of our people were no longer "free holders" and independent entrepreneurs. The tide of industrialism brought in its wake a wage-earning class and a debt-burdened agriculture. In fact, the entire superstructure of corporate industry and banking rested upon the insecure foundations of private indebtedness and a subservient working class, unprotected by organization or bargaining rights. While it is true that industry and finance are directly dependent upon the purchasing power of the masses, it is equally true that the source of income and stability of the market depend upon industry and banking. The whole economy is inextricably bound together. Sensing the magnitude of economic centralization and the mutual dependency of labor and capital, the New Deal directed its recovery efforts toward a stabilization and rejuvenation of banking, industry, and commercial farming cloaked in the security of organized labor and government regulation of business and finance.

The reform and recovery legislation may or may not have been sound. Time alone will reveal the final answer. What is significant for us lies in the recognition of the forces that prompted and promoted the program. It is a bit simplistic to say that the Depression alone gave rise to the New Deal. No doubt, the economic collapse of 1929–33 served as the primary stimulus for reform and recovery enactments. But long before the so-called Depression, farmers, labor, and social reformers had been clamoring for government to assert its power in defense of agriculture, organized labor, and the "forgotten man." That the instruments of representative government were able to ignore the voices of discontented groups is a sad commentary on democratic processes. The forces struggling for recognition had two obstacles to overcome. First, those persons in places of responsibility and leadership were disciples of a theory that "what's good for business is good for you." The substance of this theory in the minds of the political leaders of the 1920's was "what's good for business is to let business do as it pleases." The second obstacle in the path of economic readjustment for the farmer and the wage earner was their inability to bring sufficient political pressure upon the respective political parties. We may sum it up by saying that democratic processes were not functioning. Government was listening to the voice of finance and industry; agriculture and labor dissipated their energies in dissension and political apathy.

If the Depression of the early 1930's gave America the New Deal, the New Deal gave America a revitalization of democracy. The new administration opened its political ears to the multitudinous demands of the people. Let it not be forgotten that by 1933 the political situation was one of confusion and indirection. Labor, farmer, and industrialist all wanted something to be done, but none were in agreement. It rested upon the President and his advisers to direct a nation bewildered by disaster and a Congress harassed with economic panaceas. Convinced of the essential soundness of capitalistic economy and besieged by leaders of finance and industry, the New Deal first extended unprecedented financial assistance to banks and productive enterprises. It should be noted that the National Industrial Recovery Act, in its broad outlines, was a product of the political pressure of organized industry. The first Agricultural Adjustment Act bore the seal of acceptance of organized farm groups; and Section 7(a) of the N.I.R.A. found its progenitor in the American Federation of Labor and in business associations. These specific enactments are cited merely to demonstrate that American politics is essentially organized pressure politics. This is not to say that powerful pressure groups or economic forces can secure whatever they desire. In fact, by the crosscurrent of numerous forces seeking recognition, legislation such as the N.I.R.A. and A.A.A. emerges full of compromises and unrelated amendments.[25] Then, too, one cannot ignore the effect of presidential leadership. In a situation full of un-

---

[25] For example, the "inflation" amendment to the A.A.A. and Section 7(a) to N.I.R.A. giving labor the unhampered right to organize.

certainty, the New Deal philosophers were able to direct the course of legislation, thereby answering the needs of both recovery and reform. If industry was to be saved by financial aid, the giver sought to curb the abuses which had necessitated such aid. Stock market regulation, public utility control, banking reform, and numerous other correctives were given to the patient—all of this being made palatable by the soothing syrup of vast credit outlays. Thus, we see pressure group politics being directed for the public interest by the use of the spending power. Without direct coercion, an economy of diverse economic interests was cleverly organized.

Tenant farmers and unorganized labor are not powerful articulate economic forces in our political system. These groups have numbers, but not direction and organization. Their wants and hopes are not acted upon until the other more powerful pressures are satisfied. It should be recognized by the most naïve member of our society that a highly organized minority group frequently is the main force in political action. This is especially true if the majority is apathetic and broken by dissension. The American farmer has had to learn this painful lesson and today the farm interests stand out as one of the strongest political pressures in American politics. It would be carrying the argument to extremes to say that pressure politics alone is responsible for political action. The principle of political leadership and direction on the part of administrators and party chieftains invariably alters the course of "special-interest" legislation. An administration unsympathetic to the demands of labor or the farmer may resist their demands and bend its efforts for the benefit of finance and industry. American political history is resplendent with such examples. Then again, an administration such as the New Deal may encourage the growth of political pressures by lending a sympathetic ear to the hopes and aspirations of emerging interests. The New Deal has unquestionably promoted the rising power of organized labor and farm interests. It has likewise sought to curb the influence of high finance by its rather rigid control over banking and credit facilities.

The question which arises from all of this sudden development and consolidation of economic pressure is whether democratic government can survive the continuous stress and strain of powerful conflicting interests. If it is possible to force a collapse of democratic processes under the clash of numerous political and economic parties, is there not a greater danger in the failure of agriculture and labor to organize and protect itself from the rising power of corporate capitalism? The New Deal has sensed the greatest danger in the latter. Convinced that mass-production industry necessitates big business in all of its meaning, it has sought to establish a new relationship between government and people. Rather than have government directly control industry, labor, and agriculture, it has encouraged a system of checks and balances within the economic structure. This has been done by attempting to equalize the economic and political power of all groups. It has sought to make an appeal from the clamor of many private and selfish interests to the ideal of public interest.[26] President Roosevelt has

[26] Franklin D. Roosevelt, annual message to Congress, January 3, 1936, in *The Public Papers and Addresses*, V, 13.

clearly stated the philosophy of the new democracy: "Our aim was to build upon essentially democratic institutions, seeking all the while the adjustment of burdens, the help of the needy, the protection of the weak, the liberation of the exploited and the genuine protection of the people's property." [27]

[27] *Ibid.*

CHAPTER 3

A Theory of Government

LONG BEFORE the presidential campaign of 1932, Mr. Roosevelt had emerged as the leading Democratic exponent of a modern liberalism of which the kernel was the readiness to use the power of government to redress the balance of the economic world. He advocated few startling innovations, but his work at Albany had been a steadily expanding application of this twentieth-century liberalism.[1] Both as governor and as President, he based his whole philosophy of government upon one fundamental fact which seems to have escaped or has been ignored by the majority of political leaders of our time. As he put it himself, "What I emphasize, what I plead recognition for, is the fact that in the thirty years of the twentieth century more vital changes in the whole structure of civilization have taken place than

---

[1] Lindley, *The Roosevelt Revolution*, 11.

in the three hundred years which went before." [2] In other words, Mr. Roosevelt is not only aware that the social order has changed, but also that the most significant changes have come during the present century. As early as 1928, Mr. Roosevelt went out of his way to challenge the popular axiom that "the best government is the least government," saying, "The nation or state which is unwilling by governmental action to tackle new problems caused by immense increase of population and the astounding strides of modern science is headed for a decline and ultimate death from inaction." [3] In the golden era of the twenties, such a remark branded the speaker as a visionary radical. Mr. Roosevelt not only talked a more vigorous and positive use of government for the protection and control of man and business, but also, as governor of the state of New York, he carried forward his words in the form of utility regulation, labor laws, housing legislation, public works, and other forms of social legislation.[4]

It is interesting to note that Mr. Roosevelt, true to progressive traditions, has regarded the state as synonymous with the government. That is, the state is the political organization of the people; it is not the counterpart of society, but in Lockian terms is the organized government serving as trustee of society. Addressing the New York state legislature, Mr. Roosevelt gave to the record a concise statement as to his understanding of the institution known as the state: "What is the State? It is the duly constituted

[2] Quoted from one of Mr. Roosevelt's campaign speeches in 1932, *ibid.*, 10.
[3] Lindley, *Half Way with Roosevelt*, 55.
[4] Franklin D. Roosevelt, *The Public Papers and Addresses*, I, 3–8.

representative of an organized society of human beings, created by them for their mutual protection and well-being. The State or the Government is but the machinery through which such mutual aid and protection are achieved." [5]

Surely Mr. Roosevelt is here speaking in the best of liberal tradition; the words would have been familiar to any eighteenth-century politician. The duty of the state toward the citizen is the duty of the servant to the master. The people have created it; the people by common consent permit its continued existence.[6] At this point, Mr. Roosevelt leaves the past and pushes forward into a future course of government policy: "I assert that modern society, acting through government, owes the definite obligation to prevent the starvation or the dire want of any of its fellow men and women who try to maintain themselves but cannot. . . . To these unfortunate citizens aid must be extended by Government, not as a matter of charity, but as a matter of social duty." [7] The words "social duty" on the part of government are worthy of consideration. Poor relief in the bygone days had not been looked upon as a social duty but as public charity. Laissez faire government had no place within its theory for public expenditure for unemployment relief. The Hoover administration had stated repeatedly that the "dole" was un-American and demoralizing—beyond the scope of government's power and the sure road to national bankruptcy. When Mr. Roosevelt became Chief Executive, he and his administration, casting aside lip service to laissez faire government, entered upon a

[5] *Ibid.*, 485.
[6] *Ibid.*, 459.
[7] *Ibid.*

policy of government responsibility for the health, safety, and well-being of the people.

The New Deal has stated its position as to the purpose of government in no uncertain terms: "The legitimate object of government is to do for the people what needs to be done but which they cannot by individual effort do at all, or do so well, for themselves." [8] Government was not instituted to serve merely as an impersonal public instrument to be called into use after irreparable damage has been done. The President has maintained that "if we limit government to the functions of merely punishing the criminal after crimes have been committed, of gathering up the wreckage of society after the devastation of an economic collapse, or of fighting a war that reason might have prevented, then government fails to satisfy those urgent human purposes, which, in essence, gave it its beginning and provide its present justification." [9]

Modern government, in the eyes of the New Deal exponents, has become an instrument of public power through which citizens may apply their reasoned methods of prevention in addition to methods of correction. To regard government as both a corrective and a preventive force opens the way for widespread state activity. It is in line with this policy that the New Deal has invested millions of dollars in slum clearance, soil erosion control, public health services, and all forms of public welfare. The state has

[8] Abraham Lincoln, quoted in Roosevelt's address at Worcester, Mass., October 21, 1936, *ibid.*, V, 524.

[9] Franklin D. Roosevelt, message to the Fifth Annual Women's Conference on Current Problems, October 17, 1935, in *The Public Papers and Addresses*, IV, 422.

taken a new place in the life of the society from which it arises. No longer is it merely the policeman and the census-taker; the New Deal assumes the role of the philosopher king, but a constitutionally limited and democratically controlled "king," who in his accumulated wisdom directs the course to the good life.

Aristotle saw the ethical purpose of the state as the "good life." He believed man desired happiness above all else, and it was through the state that he attained it. It may be futile to try to claim that the New Deal conception of the state is Aristotelian. Surely not, but happiness and the good life are for the New Dealer, as for Aristotle, the purpose of government.

We may find a closer analogy in the political philosophy of T. H. Green, who saw the state or government as a huge reservoir of power that should be used to equalize conditions in order to provide each individual with the opportunity of self-realization. Mr. Roosevelt came remarkably close to the philosophy of Green when he remarked, "Good government should maintain the balance where every individual may have a place if he will take it; where every individual may find safety if he wishes it; where every individual may attain such power as his ability permits, consistent with his assuming the accompanying responsibility." [10]

Herein is an interpretation of governmental functions that embodies the essence of a liberal society. It makes the common good available not to a privileged class but to all,

[10] Franklin D. Roosevelt, *Looking Forward*, 9.

so far as the capacity of each permits him to share it.[11] While laying emphasis on the use of government's authority for the common good, the New Deal has not made governmental power an end in itself, but a means toward the fulfillment of the democratic objective—to increase the powers and capacities of the individual in order that he may more abundantly contribute to the common good. The aim is to so adjust conditions and burdens as to release the individual for creative effort. Government seeks to equalize privileges, not abolish them. Convinced of the dignity of the individual and confident as to the ability of the common man, the New Deal government aims at releasing the human energies of the millions burdened with poverty, debt, and insecurity.

President Roosevelt sees the task of government as that of application and encouragement.[12] A wise government "seeks to provide the opportunity through which the best individual achievement can be obtained, while at the same time it seeks to remove such obstruction, such unfairness as springs from selfish human motives."[13] Government is no longer to be a laissez faire government, exercising traditional and more or less impersonal powers. There must exist in the nation's capital a sense of responsibility for the health, safety, and welfare of the whole people. As Harold L. Ickes has written, "We are not here merely to endure a purgatorial existence in anticipation of a beatific eternity

[11] G. H. Sabine, *The History of Political Theory* (New York: H. Holt and Co., 1937), 673.
[12] Franklin D. Roosevelt, speech in San Diego, October 2, 1935, in *The Public Papers and Addresses*, IV, 406.
[13] *Ibid.*, 406–407.

after the grave closes on us. We are here with the hopes and aspirations and legitimate desires that we are entitled to have satisfied to at least a reasonable degree," [14] and if by unforeseen circumstances, the individual cannot by his own powers attain a reasonable degree of security and happiness, then government must so order society as to make that legitimate aspiration and desire a reality.

The problem that has confronted the New Deal is essentially that which has fallen on every modern nation—the proper use and control of good advancements in science, technology, and industrial development. No doubt the machine age has served well the men and women who use its products. The problem is to see that the machine age serves equally well the men and women who run the machines. If modern government, then, is to justify itself, it must see to it that human values are not mangled and destroyed.[15] The ideal embodied in such a philosophy places upon government the responsibility of caring for the hungry, the unemployed, and the dispossessed. It implies much more than mere temporary relief in the form of food and clothing; it demands of government such a reordering of the economy that the citizen may reclaim his place and function in society. Such a reordering of the economic system constitutes a challenge to democratic institutions. We may put the issue in these terms: Can the "plain people" of America, with the aid of socially minded experts and leaders, build up planfully and peacefully a new economic and political equilibrium based not upon concepts of totalitari-

14 Ickes, *The New Democracy*, 60–61.
15 Franklin D. Roosevelt, campaign address in Harrisburg, Pa., October 29, 1936, in *The Public Papers and Addresses*, V, 550–51.

anism, but on broad and flexible principles which aim to
reconcile popular control with governmental leadership,
individual efficiency with group responsibility, economic
security with orderly change, and social solidarity with a
realistic freedom? [16] The answer to this question may spell
the fate of modern democracy. If the New Deal can succeed even imperfectly in proving that democratic government can so order its economy as to provide security as
well as freedom for its people, it will have achieved great-
ness. The task required of the New Deal, as of any modern
democratic government, is to prove that democracy can be
made to function in the world of today as effectively as in
the simpler world of a hundred years ago. Modern problems demand more than the mere arguing of theory. The
times require "the confident answer of performance to
those whose instinctive faith in humanity made them want
to believe that in the long run democracy would prove
superior to more extreme forms of government as the
process of getting action when action was wisdom, without the spiritual sacrifices which those other forms of government exact." [17]

The modern democratic statesman realizes now more
than ever before that if government is to be able to meet
its appointed tasks, it must become more practical, more
efficient, and more responsive to needs. Simple honesty in
the carrying out of plans or policies is not enough. So far
as government is concerned with any social or economic

[16] Lewis L. Lorwin, "The Social Aspects of the Planning State,"
American Political Science Review, XXVIII (1934), 24.
[17] Franklin D. Roosevelt, annual message to Congress, June 6, 1937,
in *The Public Papers and Addresses*, V, 635.

planning, success can be and will be imperiled if we do not put our governmental organization in order for this duty.[18] Accordingly, the New Deal has emphasized the use of technicians, experts, and Brain Trusters. The President's attempts and partial success in an overall reorganization of the executive branch of the government have been in line with the New Deal's belief that government in the modern service state must be equipped for prompt and efficient action.

However, mere organization alone will not give democratic government the answer to the perplexing problems of finance and industrial capitalism. A new set of values is vitally necessary. Social purpose must be substituted for acquisitive ends. In other words, the measure of successful control and restoration of a stable society lies in the extent that government is willing to apply social values in place of pecuniary values. The state under the New Deal is attempting to promote the realization of this ethical purpose. Mr. Roosevelt has stated on many occasions that happiness lies not in the mere possession of money; it lies in the joy of achievement, in the thrill of creative effort. "The joy and moral stimulation to work no longer must be forgotten in the mad chase of profit. These dark days will be worth all they cost us if they teach us that our true destiny is not to be ministered unto but to minister to ourselves and our fellow men." [19]

It is all too clear that we must develop new agencies of human cooperation to meet the new economic conditions

[18] Franklin D. Roosevelt, *Looking Forward*, 71.
[19] *Ibid.*, 263.

produced by the industrial revolution. But the New Deal and its leader have recognized that it is pathetically absurd to suggest that we can create these new agencies in a year or that we can perfect them within a decade. It has been the contention of President Roosevelt that we must begin a long, slow process of trial and error, the statement and restatement of principles, the building and rebuilding of organizations equipped for public service, the writing and rewriting of administrative law, the gradual development of a public understanding and seasonal support of principles and procedures.[20] Without the exercise of foresight and without application of the best technical information available, the economic life of a complex society will likely experience severe periodic difficulties. At the same time, unless the common man, the everyday citizen, is directly associated with the exercise of foresight and the application of the technique, he will come more and more to live under a policy that is not of his own making. It was with this thought in mind that the New Deal in its agricultural program relied upon state and local committees of farmers. These committees have offered the farmers of the United States an opportunity to strengthen the democratic process, while working out national policy at the point where national policy closely touches their lives.[21] The great danger of executive leadership and New Deal practices lies in the deadening influence it may have on individual initiative and

[20] Donald R. Richberg, "Constitutional Aspects of the New Deal," *Annals of the American Academy of Political and Social Sciences,* CLXXVIII (1935), 31.

[21] F. F. Elliott, "We the People," *Land Policy Review* (May–June, 1939), 1–2.

responsiveness. If the citizen feels that government can do all for him, that he need not worry for the morrow, then the aim of releasing individual creativeness has been defeated. The task of the service state is one of challenging proportions—it may in its humanitarianism resolve itself into a bureaucracy saddled on the backs of a spineless, complacent people; it may in its desire for public good become dictatorial; it may in its desire to achieve balance and a sense of equal opportunity produce stagnation and apathy. The safety of democratic society rests in eternal vigilance on the part of its members, and this spirit of inquisitiveness must be nourished as much as the bodily security of the individual. The service state must not become the servile state.

Many changes will be required before efficient democratic government is assured; this the New Deal readily admits. The greatest and most pressing need at the present time is public understanding, education in the social purposes of democracy, and it is for government to lead the way. Mr. Roosevelt has consistently maintained that government includes more than the art of formulating policy. Its main support rests in the using of political technique to attain so much of that policy as will receive general support; "persuading, leading, sacrificing, teaching always, because the greatest duty of a statesman is to educate." [22] Mr. Roosevelt has been the personification of that statement. His every effort has been to achieve as much as possible of social reform as would seem to be consistent with the

[22] Franklin D. Roosevelt, Commonwealth Club speech, San Francisco, September 23, 1932, in *The Public Papers and Addresses*, I, 756.

capacity and willingness of those who are to be governed to
absorb the education he has given.[23] The use of the radio,
the unprecedented release of pamphlets, periodicals, and
government bulletins have all been part of the educational
program. The use of the talking moving picture in such
films as *The River* and *The Plow that Broke the Plains* are
further examples of the new techniques employed in the
process of educating a people for social democracy. For to
provide a strong and secure basis for a lasting civilization,
the new democratic movement must be founded not on
propaganda or regimentation, but on the steady growth of
real understanding among the people and on real participation by them in discussion and planning and in the execu-
tion of policies that affect their lives. True democracy
must rest on tolerance and honest thinking. Informed public opinion, based upon growing knowledge and courageous
facing of facts, is the only safe foundation.

The New Deal's accomplishments have been great, but
most fundamental of all, it has revived faith in the democratic system of government by proving that it was not
helpless in the face of a great crisis. It was left to the administration of President Roosevelt to adopt for the first
time as a national policy the theory that the country as a
whole ought to be developed and used for the greatest good
of the greatest number and that we cannot develop and use
it unless we have thoroughly and intelligently studied the
entire country—studying the people and their needs, and
planning for the fulfillment of those needs in terms of our

[23] David Lawrence, *Beyond the New Deal* (New York: McGraw-
Hill Book Co., 1934), 303.

resources.[24] Not only has the New Deal believed that the country as a whole ought to be used and developed for all people, but it has viewed the country itself as a unit, a sort of organic society. The government policy has been stated as a "concert of interests"—North, South, East, and West; agriculture, industry, commerce, and finance.[25] It is the problem of government, says Mr. Roosevelt, to harmonize the interests of these groups, which are often divergent and opposing—to harmonize them in order to guarantee security for as many of their individual members as may be possible. "The science of politics, indeed, may properly be said to be in large part the science of the adjustment of conflicting group interests." [26] Thus we see the New Deal recognizing a sort of pluralistic nature of society. However, it does not see society as an aggregate of equal groups, for in the federal government, says the President, the problem is to adjust "still greater groups in the interests of the largest group of all—a hundred and twenty-five million people in whom reposes the sovereignty of the United States." [27] The whole of society takes on a significance here which challenges any individualistic selfishness or egoism. The President reminds us that the individual citizen contributes most to the good of this largest group only when he or she thinks in terms of the largest group.[28] As a matter of fact, it has been approximately stated that Mr. Roosevelt himself went to work in Washington somewhat

[24] Ickes, *The New Democracy*, 96.
[25] Franklin D. Roosevelt, *Looking Forward*, 241.
[26] Franklin D. Roosevelt, address at Rollins College, Florida, March 23, 1936, in *The Public Papers and Addresses*, V, 148.
[27] *Ibid.*
[28] *Ibid.*, 149.

under the spell of the pleasant idea that we were all just one great happy family, and he persisted in his philosophy in spite of group attacks on him or his policies.[29] The words from an important address given in 1936 are conclusive: "We have no separate interests in America. There is nothing to say to one group that ought not be said to all groups. What is good for one ought to be good for all. We can make our machinery of private enterprise work only so long as it does not benefit one group at the expense of another." [30]

It would not be wrong to say that the New Deal has repudiated the conception of society as one made of autonomous independent individuals. The cruel suffering of the recent Depression has impressed upon us unforgettable lessons—lessons of which the administration in Washington took notice. We have been compelled by stark necessity to unlearn the too-comfortable superstition that the American soil was mystically blessed with immunity to economic maladjustments and that the American spirit of "rugged individualism"—unhelped by the cooperative efforts of government—could withstand and repel every form of economic disarrangement or crisis.[31] The severity of the recent Depression has demonstrated that no one group or class in our society is immune from the forces which overwhelm the general community. It is this feeling of interdependence that the New Deal has attempted to promote. It has sought to substitute the general good in place of the

[29] Lindley, *Half Way with Roosevelt*, 419.
[30] Franklin D. Roosevelt, *The Public Papers and Addresses*, V, 534.
[31] Franklin D. Roosevelt, address to Young Democrats' clubs, August 24, 1935, in *The Public Papers and Addresses*, IV, 338–39.

old philosophy of individual self-interest and group selfishness. It has sought to make government responsible to all the people in this country, turning the national power into a great national crusade to destroy enforced idleness and poverty. American business, agriculture, and labor were to think less of their own profit and more of the national functions they perform. Each unit must think of itself as part of a greater whole, one piece in a large design. The President's words represent the new attitude: "America is an economic unit. New means and methods of transportation and communication have made us economically as well as politically a single nation. . . . All that this Administration has done, all that it proposes to do—and this it does propose to do—is to use every power and authority of the Federal government to protect the commerce of America from the selfish forces which ruined it. . . . Your Government has but one sign on its desk—seek only the greater good of the greater number of Americans." [32]

[32] Franklin D. Roosevelt, address in Chicago, October 14, 1936, in *The Public Papers and Addresses*, V, 483.

CHAPTER 4

A More Perfect Union

"The Constitution was intended to endure for the ages and consequently to be adapted to the various crises of human affairs." Herein lies the proposition that has caused no end of argument concerning the powers and nature of American government. Two interpretations have consistently clouded the political horizon. First, is the Constitution to be considered as a static symbol of an established order? Or, secondly, is it to be looked upon and used as an instrument of power for the common welfare, as that welfare may be determined by the majority of the body politic? The affirmative acceptance of the latter position by the New Deal precipitated one of the most bitter political struggles in American constitutional history.

Long-drawn-out battles as to the meaning, purpose, and powers embodied in the Constitution are more American than the Constitution itself. Just as surely as the major outlines of American constitutional government flow from

British sources, judicial and executive controversy over matters of constitutional power find their roots in the famous argument between King James and Lord Coke. British as our political ancestry may be, no one has ever surpassed the originality and poignancy of American controversies as to what the Constitution means and what powers it gives to the national government.

The history of the first century of our national existence records numerous constitutional debates of momentous importance. The issue of "state rights" rang through the halls of Congress until the issue was finally settled on the battlefields of Gettysburg and Atlanta. With the question of secession squelched by the force of arms, the arena of constitutional debate tended to drift in the direction of economic issues. Southern agrarianism had lost its dominant position in the struggle for economic and political power. Northern industrialism and its copartner, high finance, guided the destinies of the young republic. The accepted policy for government in its relationship to business was bluntly put at "hands off." It was not until the disappearance of the frontier in the late 1890's that the heart of constitutional debate reached significant intensity. The explanation for the political apathy of the thirty years following the Civil War seems to be found in the superabundance of free land and the expansive development of industrial plant. Just so long as a safety valve for economic maladjustment existed in the form of new land and expanding work opportunities, the problem of the Constitution and its relationship to government control of business was never examined. This is to say, the Constitution was not allowed to stand in the way of expansion or acquisition of property rights.

The function of the Constitution in the first century of our nationhood was that of securing sufficient allegiance to the union to preserve a national spirit. It was not allowed to interfere in any manner with the conquering of a continent.[1] It will further clarify the position of the Constitution in our early years of national life if we remember that its prime objective was to protect property, and since everyone or almost everyone had property or easy access to it, everyone revered and respected the memorable document. It also should be noted that when our constitutions, both federal and state, were written, the tradition of the English law, the contemporary political philosophy, and the economic situation of the American democracy all conspired to embody in them and their interpretation "an extremely individualistic conception of justice—a conception which practically confided social welfare to the free expression of individual interests and individual good intentions."[2] Such an interpretation was in tune with the best interest of the people because of the decentralized nature of the economy and the necessity for broad play of individual initiative in the conquering of the frontier and the expansion of the nation's power.

The growth of corporations and the ever-increasing concentration of wealth and property in the hands of a minority of the population had reached substantial proportions by the late 1890's and early 1900's. It is true that while

[1] Herbert Croly, *Progressive Democracy* (New York: Macmillan Co., 1914), 150–60.
[2] *Ibid.*, 148.

fewer people were blessed with the privilege of property, and while our economy became highly industrialized, bringing in its wake an increasing number of wage earners and tenant farmers, the old individualistic interpretation of the Constitution was strictly adhered to. Much to the pleasure and benefit of the new crop of millionaires and industrial leaders, the institution of property known as a corporation was cloaked in all the rights and privileges of a person, thereby extending to corporate wealth the protections of "life, liberty, and property" as guaranteed by the Fifth and Fourteenth Amendments. The courts refused to recognize the impersonal nature of a corporation, that it was but a creature of the state; and that to extend the protections and privileges intended for an individual to a financial or industrial combine on the same basis as to a human being was not equal protection of the laws, but gross inequality and favoritism. Such an interpretation of the constitutional protections carried with it a demolishing limitation of the federal government's power to regulate or control corporate practices. Corporations were deemed "citizens" of the state. Thus, the application of the prohibitions and limitations on the state police power, as embodied in the due process clause of the Fourteenth Amendment, restricted state control over corporate business to a bare minimum. In other words, the new grants of finance and industry were literally free from any control, except in the most obvious and pernicious instances.[3]

The reaction to the growth of monopolies and huge in-

---

[3] See the constitutional law cases: *U.S.* v. *E. C. Knight Co.* (1895) 156 U.S. 1; *Pollock* v. *Farmers' Loan and Trust Co.* (1895) 158 U.S. 601; antitrust cases.

dustrial and financial combinations blossomed forth in the antitrust laws and in a frontal assault by the Populists and later the Bull Moose Party on the conservatism of the Supreme Court. However, no one challenged the sacredness and the justice of the Constitution. The trouble was not in the document, but in the "nine old men" whose duty and prerogative it was to apply and interpret the written word. All sorts of schemes were devised to curb the powers of the Court, but, as usual, nothing came of the uproar, except a temporary relaxing by the Court of its essential conservatism.

Having summarily considered the background of the interpretations placed upon the Constitution by a century and a half of judicial practice, it is necessary to clarify a most important question: namely, what is the Constitution? It has been stated most appropriately that the "Constitution is what the judges say it is," [4] and here we have the issue that has caused the New Deal no end of difficulty, embarrassment, and jubilation. Whether or not we agree with any of the attempts to define the Constitution, there is a point of compromise which should satisfy every critic. The Constitution is a declaration of fundamental political and social principles. It is subject to interpretation. As time goes on, it expands here and contracts there. If it were incapable of growth it would long ago have become a dead and lifeless thing. "It would have been discarded long since by an expanding society of free born, liberty loving Americans if they had not been able to adjust it to their changing

[4] Statement by Charles Evans Hughes.

needs." [5] With this statement in mind, we may study the constitutional theory of the New Deal and attempt to find out if the New Deal has, as its critics say, "scrapped the Constitution and captured the judiciary." [6]

Edward S. Corwin, one of our leading students and authorities on the Constitution, has divided the study of the Constitution into four categories—as a document, as a law, as a symbol, and as an instrument. As a *document* the Constitution came from its framers and its elaboration was an event of the greatest historical interest.[7] But as a *law* the Constitution comes from and derives all of its force from the people of the United States of this day and hour.[8] In the words of the Preamble: "We the people of the United States, *do* ordain and establish this Constitution"—not *did* ordain and establish. The Constitution is thus always in contact with and part of the source of its being—the people. It is a living statute to be interpreted in the light of living conditions. It should be interpreted as "palpitating with the purpose of the hour, re-enacted with every waking breath of the American people, whose primitive right to determine their institutions is its sole claim to validity as a law and as the matrix of laws under our system." [9] No doubt the Constitution should offer resistance to the too-easy triumph of social forces, but it must be only the resistance of its words when they have been fairly construed from a point of view which is sympa-

---

[5] Ickes, *The New Democracy*, 43.
[6] David Lawrence, "The Revolution," 16.
[7] E. S. Corwin, "Constitution v. Constitutional Theory," *American Political Science Review*, XIX (1925), 302.
[8] *Ibid.*
[9] *Ibid.*, 303.

thetic with "the aspirations of the existing generation of American people, rather than that which is furnished by concern for theories as to what was intended by a generation long since dissolved in its native dust." [10]

The Constitution as a *symbol* is best described in that well-known phrase "What is, is right." In other words, by some peculiar twist of the mind, certain people and well-established interests decide that the day for constitutional interpretation and expansion is over. The millennium of constitutional purity and sacredness has arrived and any efforts to demand a revised or an extended interpretation of constitutional powers is treason and blasphemy. The aspect of the Constitution as a symbol and bulwark of a previously achieved order of human rights appears most clearly in the rantings of the Liberty League and the statements of such auspicious organizations as the Chamber of Commerce and the National Association of Manufacturers. In the eyes of the "symbolists," no longer must the Constitution be looked upon as a living document but, much better, as a holy writ, the chief purpose of which is to protect those who are blessed with a superabundance of property and leisure. According to Mr. Ickes, there has grown up in this country a special breed of constitutional symbolists, namely, the great constitutional lawyers.[11] They regard the Constitution as something negative, as an instrument with which to block, if possible, but in any event to obstruct any social advance. "They are professional 'viewers with alarm'; they suffer all their lives from the

[10] *Ibid.*, 302.
[11] Ickes, *The New Democracy*, 46.

'misery'; they are never so happy as when they are unhappy and they are never so unhappy as when someone
attempts to do something for the benefit of mankind." [12]
Mr. Ickes believes the symbolist constitutional lawyer sees
the Constitution as a veto power that may not be over-
ridden even by the people whose instrument it is. It is not
a human, living instrumentality for social growth.

The aspect of the Constitution of the United States as an
instrument of popular government for the achievement of
great ends of social growth is stamped on its opening
words: "We the people of the United States, in order to
form a more perfect union, establish justice, insure domestic tranquillity, provide for the common defense, promote the general welfare, and secure the blessings of liberty
to *ourselves* and our *posterity* do ordain and establish this
Constitution for the United States of America." [13] It is this
interpretation that has provided the basis for the New Deal
philosophy of government. It is not to be supposed that
the Preamble is a grant of power, but rather it is a recita-
tion of the purposes, or a catalogue of the ultimate ends to
be served by the powers granted in the Constitution itself.
"No gloss derived from speculative theories about the
nature of the Union should have ever been permitted to
obscure its clear import." [14] Such phrases as to "secure the
blessings of liberty to *ourselves* and our *posterity*" assert the
living, vital nature of the powers granted and to the modern mind can mean little less than that the delegated powers
are to be exercised in direct ratio to the magnitude, com-

[12] *Ibid.*, 47.
[13] Preamble of the Constitution.
[14] Corwin, "Constitution v. Constitutional Theory," 302.

plexity, and nature of the problem to be solved. To those who see the Constitution as an instrument of power, not a negation of it, adequate authority lies within the document to meet the demands of modern problems as they arise. The New Deal has embraced this interpretation.

Homer S. Cummings, former United States attorney general, has stated the entire proposition which long confounded the New Deal: "The real difficulty is not with the Constitution but with the judges who interpret it." [15] Here we see no criticism of the Constitution. In fact, Mr. Roosevelt and his aides are patriotic defenders of the document. Repeatedly, in public pronouncements and in messages to Congress, the President has declared that there is little fault to be found with the Constitution.[16] "The vital need is not an alteration of our fundamental law, but an increasingly enlightened view with reference to it. Difficulties have grown out of its interpretation; but rightly considered, it can be used as an instrument of progress, and not as a device for prevention of action." [17] Most New Deal theorists and constitutional lawyers rely upon evidence presented in the debates in the constitutional convention. Mr. Roosevelt is convinced from his study of the debates and notes that the members of the convention were fully aware that civilization would raise new problems for the then proposed federal government which they themselves could not even surmise, and that it was their definite

[15] Carl Brent Swisher (ed.), *Selected Papers of Homer Cummings* (New York: Charles Scribner's Sons, 1939), 121.
[16] Franklin D. Roosevelt, annual message to Congress, January 6, 1937, in *The Public Papers and Addresses*, V, 639.
[17] *Ibid.*

intent and expectation that a liberal interpretation in the years to come would give the Congress the same relative powers over new national problems as they themselves gave to the Congress over the national problems of their day.[18] The words of Edmund Randolph are the New Dealers' favorite text for their constitutional philosophy. It was the purpose "to insert essential principles only, lest the operation of government should be clogged by rendering those provisions permanent and unalterable which ought to be accommodated to times and events." [19] Add to this the remark attributed to Jefferson that "no society can make a perpetual constitution or even a perpetual law," [20] and it can be readily seen that the New Dealers are not without respectable and truly American company in their argument.

Perhaps the major part of the New Deal program has been based upon the power of Congress to regulate interstate commerce. The history of the trend toward federal centralization is very largely the history of the commerce power.[21] The grant of power remains the same, but the content of the term *commerce* and the methods and policies which constitute "regulation" have tended to keep pace with the growing complexities of modern life. Interstate commerce has been interpreted to include virtually every form of intercourse across a state line, whether it be by rail, boat, radio, automobile, or airplane; and the power to

---

[18] *Ibid.,* 640.
[19] Quote from Edmund Randolph by President Roosevelt, *ibid.,* 639.
[20] Vernon Louis Parrington, *Main Currents in American Thought* (3 vols.; New York: Harcourt, Brace and Co., 1927–30), II, 12.
[21] *The Supreme Court and the Constitution,* Public Affairs Pamphlet No. 7 (New York: Public Affairs Committee, 1937), 5.

regulate that commerce has been interpreted to include the power to make the rules by which it is carried on, to promote or protect it, or to prohibit it from being used for purposes of public injury. The power given is over foreign and interstate commerce and does not extend to commerce carried on wholly within a state. However, in some cases purely local transactions which may or do obstruct or affect interstate commerce have been declared subject to regulation by the federal government.[22] It is only a step from this to the theory that the commercial and industrial life of the nation is a unit, so that Congress is still regulating interstate commerce when it strikes at abuses superficially local in character. This has been the philosophy of the New Deal as to the scope of the commerce power. It is a philosophy made vital by the economic collapse in the early 1930's, and receives its empirical proof from the well-recognized fact that an economic disaster in any business in one part of the country had direct repercussions in some distant place. New Dealers view the economic life of the nation as a coordinated organism.

It was on the liberal interpretation of the commerce clauses that the New Deal based the N.I.R.A., the Guffey Coal Conservation Act, and the Railroad Retirement Act— all of which were subsequently declared unconstitutional.[23]

[22] *Illinois Central Railroad Co.* v. *Illinois* (1896) 163 U.S. 142. (A state law requiring all railroads to stop at all county seats seriously burdens interstate traffic.) In the *Shreveport* case (1914) 234 U.S. 342, state freight rates were held to injure interstate commerce because state rates were so low as to discriminate against interstate shipping.

[23] *Schechter* v. *U.S.* (1935) 295 U.S. 495, the N.R.A. case; *Railroad Retirement Board* v. *Alton Railroad Co.* (1935) 295 U.S. 330; *Carter* v. *Carter Coal Co.* (1936) 298 U.S. 201.

An even greater blow to the New Deal attempts for economic recovery was delivered by the Court in a six-to-three
decision in the instance of the Agricultural Adjustment
Act, wherein the Court held that a misuse of the taxing
power was evident and that agriculture is a local industry
not subject to federal regulation.[24] The action of the Court
in these early New Deal decisions literally stripped the
administration of its program and seriously impaired any
attempt for economic recovery or reform legislation. It was
in his celebrated "horse and buggy" press conference, after
the invalidation of the National Recovery Administration,
that Mr. Roosevelt said bluntly that the issue presented was
whether or not the national government was to have the
power to deal with national economic problems.[25] Every
New Deal exponent and the major portion of progressive
politicians sincerely believed that the early legislation did
not challenge the Constitution; it merely challenged the
economic practices which had been clothed with more or
less constitutional authority by the Supreme Court over a
long period of years. For nearly a half-century the tendency
of the Supreme Court, through what New Dealers termed
a rather narrow and conservative interpretation of the
commerce clause and the due process clause of the Fourteenth Amendment, had been to place a narrowing con-
struction on the powers of the federal government and a
limitation on state government. The rights of the government to protect individual citizens were being gradually
whittled away. The rights of economically powerful indi-

[24] *U.S.* v. *Butler* (1936) 297 U.S. 1.
[25] Franklin D. Roosevelt, two hundred ninth press conference, in
The Public Papers and Addresses, IV, 200.

viduals and corporations to pursue activities free from government restraint were being continuously extended. Gradually there was created an increasing area of "no-man's land" where neither the Congress nor the state legislatures could constitutionally legislate to promote the security of the average man.

The New Deal, led by the Chief Executive, openly revolted against the Court's conservative attitude. It demanded that the Court recognize that the American experiment required liberal interpretation of the interstate commerce and due process clauses and an enlargement of the idea of a public utility.[26] The President contended that the general welfare clause of the Constitution should be construed broadly to include anything conducive to the national welfare, unaffected by the specifically enumerated powers which follow the clause "that, pursuant to it, the Congress may raise taxes and appropriate the proceeds to promote the general welfare."[27] The New Deal further urged that the determination of what was a national purpose rests with the Congress and not with the courts and that the Court should take notice of the interdependence of the several units in our national economy and forget the "horse and buggy" days.[28] Mr. Roosevelt reminded the people that the men who addressed themselves to the task of laying the framework of our national government wrote down in enduring words that their aim was to form "a more perfect union," and in writing this ideal into the Preamble of the Constitution, they set a task for future

---

[26] Lindley, *The Roosevelt Revolution*, 317.
[27] Franklin D. Roosevelt, *The Public Papers and Addresses*, IV, 10.
[28] *Ibid.*, 10–11.

generations as well as for themselves. They (the Founding Fathers) were forming a new government suited, as they believed, "to the conditions of their day, but they were wise enough to look into the future and recognize that the conditions of life and the demands upon government were bound to change as they had been changing through ages past. So, the plan of government that they had prepared was made, not rigid but flexible—adapted to change and progress." [29] Mr. Roosevelt and his administration felt it was and is a patriotic duty to accept the responsibility of remolding government to make it more serviceable to all the people and more responsive to current needs. In that task, not only must the legislative and executive branches of the government continue to meet the demand of progressive democracy, but the judicial branch is called upon to do its part.[30] The President did not ask the courts to call nonexistent powers into being, but stated, "We have a right to expect that conceded powers or those legitimately implied shall be made effective instruments of the common good." [31] The processes of our democracy must not be imperiled by the denial of essential powers of a free government.

The battle for a liberal interpretation of constitutional powers was carried on with eloquence and persuasion. A wholehearted affection and patriotic respect were repeatedly professed for the Constitution, and, in fact, the New Dealers became the self-appointed defenders of our Amer-

[29] Franklin D. Roosevelt, *Looking Forward*, 87.
[30] Franklin D. Roosevelt, annual message to Congress, January 6, 1937, in *The Public Papers and Addresses*, V, 641.
[31] *Ibid.*

ican system. Of course, the defense was predicated upon the issue that to deny government adequate powers to control abuses and exploitation in the economic system was tantamount to issuing a death warrant for American democracy. To Mr. Roosevelt, the Constitution is a human document formulated to serve human needs; "it is the servant and not the master of those who created it." [32]

The New Deal found historical support in the supreme individualist Thomas Jefferson. He realized that there are times when a strict observance of the written law must give way to the higher obligation of observance of the laws of necessity and self-preservation. Thomas Jefferson realized "to lose our country by a scrupulous adherence to written law would be to lose the law itself, with life, liberty, and property and all those who are enjoying them with us; thus absurdly sacrificing the end to the means." [33] Although Jefferson would have condoned, in an emergency, a disregard for the letter of the written law, Charles A. Beard points out that in the New Deal, "there has not been the slightest fundamental departure from the form or the nature of our government or the established order." [34] Every new power entrusted to the President has been conferred by the people, acting through their duly elected representatives. "The Congress has neither abdicated nor shirked its rights or its duties . . . . what is really happening is not an alteration in the established form or texture of

[32] Swisher (ed.), *Selected Papers of Homer Cummings*, 177.
[33] Charles Maurice Wiltse, *The Jeffersonian Tradition in American Democracy* (Chapel Hill: University of North Carolina Press, 1935), 174.
[34] Charles A. Beard and George H. E. Smith, *The Future Comes: A Study of the New Deal* (New York: Macmillan, 1933), 155.

government, but a change in the spirit and application of government." [35]

After having given vent to his emotions in the "horse and buggy" statement, Mr. Roosevelt apparently decided to withhold his fire on the Court until after the 1936 presidential election. The overwhelming majority accorded him was interpreted as a mandate from the people for the President and his policies. This victory spurred the New Deal to renewed efforts. The courts were again asked to uphold the recovery legislation. It was suggested that a constitutional amendment should be proposed to authorize the federal government to wield extensive powers over the economic system in general. Mr. Roosevelt toyed with the idea for some weeks, but became convinced that the process of amendment was too slow to be effective in the present emergency.[36] The situation was critical for the New Deal when the Supreme Court refused to uphold legislation which, apparently, the people approved and the administration had given its promise to fulfill. All that remained of the New Deal program by early 1936 were the spending features, and even these had been endangered by the A.A.A. decision. Unless its policies could be made effective, the administration faced the prospect of discredit and failure.

Under these circumstances, and in a firm belief that the Constitution afforded ample power to meet any and all emergencies, the President in a special message to Congress proposed a reorganization of the judicial branch of the

[35] *Ibid.,* 156.
[36] Swisher (ed.), *Selected Papers of Homer Cummings,* 147–48.

government.[37] The essence of his judiciary proposal was the appointment of an additional judge for each judge of retirement age—that is, of seventy years of age or more—who failed to retire upon full salary as permitted by law. Thus, either the courts would be increased in size or, if judges of retirement age did retire, new judges would be appointed in their places. In either event, new judges, presumably of a liberal turn of mind, would be appointed. These would either overcome or supersede the conservatives of most courts, including the Supreme Court.[38] The plan precipitated a series of debates and speeches, the intensity of which had not been equalled in fifty years. The President was accused of attempting to "pack" the Court and capture the judiciary, and of trying to be a dictator. Orators wrapped themselves in Old Glory and prepared to do battle for the Founding Fathers. The amazing thing about the whole of the struggle was that precedent and reason were on the side of Roosevelt, yet the proposed bill was thoroughly defeated. Nothing is more truly American than a little tampering with the Supreme Court. Jefferson, Jackson, Lincoln, and Grant, together with the congresses of their respective periods, saw no objection to enlarging the Court. Mr. Roosevelt, up to 1937, had not been privileged to appoint a single member to the highest bench, whereas some of his predecessors had appointed as many as twelve members.[39] Furthermore, it was not un-American to have an occasional scrap with the justices; in fact, it is

[37] Franklin D. Roosevelt, message to Congress, February 5, 1937, in *The Public Papers and Addresses*, IV, 13–14.
[38] Radio speech by Homer Cummings, February 14, 1937, in Swisher (ed.), *Selected Papers of Homer Cummings*, 151.
[39] *Ibid.*, 151–52.

one of our choice bits of good rugged American history. Jefferson openly challenged innumerable Federalist judges and ignored a subpoena issued by Chief Justice Marshall. Jackson, in a stubborn moment, told the Supreme Court to try to enforce its decrees. Lincoln had challenged the Dred Scott decision and later totally disregarded Chief Justice Taney's demand that the writ of habeas corpus be restored.[40]

The President's court plan may go down in history as the most successful failure in American politics. The justices suddenly had a change of heart and proceeded to "get in line" with the New Deal policies, and to this date have yet to overrule a congressional enactment since 1936. The section of the original bill dealing with the Supreme Court has substantially served its objective by liberalizing the Court and making it immediately responsive to the national will. It has been under the tense agitation stirred by the President that the Court made its recent path-blazing interpretations of the due process, commerce, and general welfare clauses, all of which are now interpreted in line with New Deal policy. The Court has undone in two years its handiwork of a half-century; witness the frank reversal of the minimum wage cases, the reversal of the Carter coal case by the Wagner Act decision,[41] and the enlargement of the ambit of "general welfare" in the momentous social security cases,[42] which, in effect, reversed the Court's posi-

---

[40] *Ibid.*, 151.
[41] *National Labor Relations Board* v. *Jones & Laughlin Steel Corporation* (1937) 301 U.S. 1.
[42] *Carmichael* v. *Southern Coal & Coke Company* (1937) 301 U.S. 495; *Steward Machine Company* v. *Davis* (1937) 301 U.S. 548; *Helvering* v. *Davis* (1937) 301 U.S. 619.

tion in the Hoosac Mills decision that wrecked the A.A.A. Anyone who has studied some of the more recent Supreme Court reviews of the National Labor Relations Board's decisions cannot help but be impressed with the complete shifting of interpretation of the commerce clauses. Any business or economic unit, regardless of its size, if it is part of or in line with interstate commerce, is now subject to federal regulation. The economic system has become a national unit in the eyes of the Court and as such is susceptible of national control and adjustment. The social security cases have firmly placed within the sphere of government aid and assistance the aged, the sick, the unemployed, and the dependent. The power of Congress to legislate for the general welfare by use of the taxing power has been given full sanction, and the much-used device of grants-in-aid to the states has received new impetus.

The question uppermost in our minds must be, What forces or influences has this broadened interpretation of the Constitution released? There can be little doubt that the tendency toward centralization of governmental power in Washington has received unprecedented encouragement. This can be an omen of good fortune, if we look upon centralized direction and control as a means toward efficiency and democratic planning. But it may lead to an impersonal relationship between government and citizen that will be destructive of individual initiative and personal integrity. People may grow to regard government as something separate from and above them. A bureaucracy may find a firm foothold in our governmental system and cease to be responsive to the will of the people. Congress may be in the process of signing away its powers to a principle of strong executive leadership, which within itself, although not destructive of democratic principles, may give rise to a spirit of *noblesse oblige*, or paternalism, that is not conducive to a government of the people and by the people and for the people. These are all possibilities, but not necessarily probabilities. It may be that now is the time in our democratic development to release the forces of progressive democracy from the restraints and shackles of rigid constitutional limitations. It may be necessary and proper that government of the majority be allowed more freedom in the exercise of power, since the responsibility of authority can be and should be the refiner's fire for true self-government. If the New Deal, in its desire for extensive governmental action, released from the burdens of what it terms outmoded traditions and limitations, has provided a means for the full development and maturity of democracy, it has given much to the cause of freedom. It may have set in motion a cold, pragmatic philosophy that can ultimately lead to a Fascist system, wherein the immediate problem is the essence. However, with its adherence to the essential outlines of political democracy and capitalism, it may be much more plausible to view the New Deal as an attempted answer to a political and economic situation, an effort to adjust democratic principles to twentieth-century conditions.

No government or social system can experience the hardships and tribulations of a world depression without some alteration of the previous scheme of things. While the constitutional system of the pre–New Deal era remains structurally unchanged, the strides taken by government in the realm of economic control and social responsibility have undoubtedly changed the course of American politics. One need search no further than the Republican and Democratic party platforms of 1940. The outstanding factor of both was not their opposition in principles of public policy, but their essential agreement. The politics of laissez faire has given way to the dynamic philosophy of the service state. Louis M. Hacker, surveying the era of New Deal administration, summarized the program in the following words:

Our state has become transformed almost overnight. Formerly, it concerned itself almost exclusively with the civil administration and national defense, and when it intervened in other realms it for the most part acted in the capacity of umpire between equals. . . . Today, however, the state is operating to defend the underprivileged, to increase the national income, and to effect a more equitable distribution of that income among the various categories of producers . . . . Our state, in short, has become the capitalist state, where only yesterday it was the laissez-faire or passive state; it protects the young, weak and aged; it constructs and operates plants, and it buys and sells goods and services, lends money, warehouses commodities, moves ships and operates railroads. In one sense, the state is seeking to erect safeguards for the underprivileged against exploitation; in another, it is competing with and replacing private enterprise, without, however, parting company with capitalist relations.[43]

---

[43] Hacker, *American Problems of Today*, vii.

CHAPTER 5

Life—Liberty—Property

THE PROBLEM of modern democracy is intrinsically an economic one. It may be fairly stated thus: Can the flagrant inequality of possessions and of opportunity now existing in a democratic state be corrected by democratic methods? For the past decade, in the most prosperous democratic states, from 10 to 20 percent of the working population has been kept alive by government subsidy, dole, or government employment. The economic catastrophe of mass unemployment is made the more spectacular when we realize that neither natural resources and machines nor finance are lacking. On the contrary, there is wealth in abundance. Given our natural resources, manpower, and technical facilities, there could be produced in this country at least sufficient wealth to provide all the people with the necessities of life and many of the desired luxuries and comforts. Yet, in spite of widespread and insistent human need, the technical equipment has been used only in part, manpower has not been fully employed, and production has been curtailed. Obviously, the situation is one which arises not from lack of potential wealth, but from some defect, some maladjustment in the methods of producing and distributing the goods of life.

The ironic scene of want in the midst of plenty, of unemployment where there is an abundance of both capital and material, is made the more spectacular by the unprecedented attempts on the part of democratic government to control and correct the social upheaval. The economic and political doctrines of the liberal democratic ideology permitted little or no interference by government with the freedom of the individual. Political democracy and the laissez faire system of private interference grew as one. Freedom of the individual became the criterion of democratic society. The assumption was never better stated than by John Stuart Mill in his famous essay *On Liberty*. Government interference with the activities of the individual, he maintained, is never justified except when manifestly necessary to prevent the activities of some individuals from injuring others. The principle is more pointedly stated in the French Declaration of Rights of Man and of the Citizen: "Liberty is the right of everyone to do whatever does not injure others."

The liberal democratic principles of freedom found reality in both political and economic institutions. In the economic realm, this principle was interpreted to mean the maximum freedom of the individual to change his work or business and to enter freely into contracts for the acquisition or disposal of property or for the purchase or sale of personal services. It was assumed that the free play of the individual initiative motivated by the desire for profit or gain would result in the maximum production of wealth. The competitive instinct, operating through the law of supply and demand, and the resulting price system, would result in as equitable a distribution of wealth as the natural qualities and defects of men would permit.[1] In the competitive system the problem of government was reduced to guaranteeing the rights of private property, enforcing rules of contract, and preserving social order. The government was to be policeman and not otherwise to interfere with the operation of the system.

Contrary to widespread belief, laissez faire was never more than a theory imperfectly applied. The "necessary evil" of government regulation has always been with us. In fact, the institution of private property is itself a drastic regulation of business enterprise, and the law of contract an interference with the liberty of the individual. But assuming private property and the law of contract as part of the system, there was never a time when government did not find it necessary to interfere with the activities of some individuals in order to prevent those activities from injuring others. That democratic government can and has regulated the activities of certain institutions and individuals testifies to the efficacy of democratic principles, providing, however, that such regulation represents the majority will. The prevailing assumption was, and still is, in democratic states that government regulation should be kept to a minimum, however high that minimum might

---

[1] Carl L. Becker, *Modern Democracy* (New Haven: Yale University Press, 1941), 69, Chap. 3.

prove to be. The only question relevant to democratic regulation of man and property is in what ways and to what extent government should so interfere. However, the question of the means and extent of regulation cannot be considered in the terms of a mathematical calculation. It may involve not only the ways of regulation and the consideration of the extent of control, but even more important, the purpose of government action. Is the objective merely regulation or government control to check abuses and injurious practices? Or is the objective not only regulation to equalize burdens and opportunities, but also to point a new way? Has the New Deal embraced in its regulatory policies a positive social program under the direction of government? Has it the responsibility of planning along with regulation? If the answer to this question is in the affirmative, then the New Deal has clearly forsaken the negativistic political philosophy of early nineteenth-century liberalism. If we should grant that Mr. Roosevelt and his administration no longer believe in the laissez faire state or in the view that "that government is best which governs least," we must ask ourselves what will happen or has happened to those political principles of the eighteenth- and nineteenth-century liberalism— namely, the inalienable rights of life, liberty, and property? What is the effect of New Deal measures upon such ideals as individualism and freedom? Yes, the impact of New Deal politics demands an analysis of our political doctrines. What does individualism mean to the New Dealer? What is the relationship of private property to public welfare? If liberty means absence of restraint, can one call such legislation as the Wheeler-Rayburn Holding Company

Act, the soil conservation program, the wage and hour law, bulwarks of freedom? Surely Americans must re-examine their favorite political niceties and see how the New Deal has interpreted and refined them.

Such terms as *individualism*, *liberty*, and *freedom* are often used interchangeably by modern politicians and political commentators. While political theorists may write long discourses carefully distinguishing between liberty, freedom, and individualism, the layman has identified these liberal concepts or democratic principles with the simple but appropriate phrase of "absence of restraint," and more particularly the restriction of governmental authority. Americans, reared in a political atmosphere permeated with ideas that "government should keep its hands off," that all government is a necessary evil, and that any government interference with business amounts to regimentation, find themselves rather confused when so-called liberals or progressives advocate innumerable proposals giving government the authority to regulate and control all sections of the American economy. Just as Herbert Spencer revolted against the doctrines of T. H. Green and later of the nineteenth-century English liberals, so many Americans, faithful to the politics and economics of our forefathers, have resisted the regulations and restrictions of the New Deal. Is it preserving freedom, individualism, and liberty when a political program promotes and facilitates trade unions? Is it individualism when government assumes responsibility for the private well-being of millions of citizens? Is it liberty when farmers may no longer plant as much as they want to, or can no longer use their soil as they see fit? Is it preserving private enterprise when government not only regulates profits, wages, and hours, but also actually competes, as in the public utility industry? These and the innumerable other questions are being asked concerning the New Deal's faith to traditional American political principles.

Mr. Roosevelt and his advisers have refused to divorce political principles from economic realities. It is here that the confusion as to the meaning of individualism and liberty takes place. If society remained static, if man's economic institutions and social relationships were unchangeable, then definitions of political principles might be definite. However, if we are willing to concede that the American doctrine of individual liberty had its origin in economic conditions widely different from those which prevail to-day, there may be a justification for a redefinition of old political concepts. Individual liberty surrounded by the reality of an unconquered frontier may mean one thing, but in the age of the modern mass-assembly factory it may mean something quite different. Government policy and action must be judged not in the vacuum of imagined situations but in the harsh reality of existing conditions. Governments are not thought out in abstraction but spring from practical needs and if they are to endure they must meet the requirements of practice. In other words, the final test of good government is the pragmatic test. No philosophy of the state, therefore, can be made intelligible without some comprehension of the social, economic, and intellectual forces out of which it arose.

To condemn or praise New Deal programs by a simple comparison with the days of 1800 is neither scientific nor reasonable. Government in 1800 was appropriate for that day and the needs of the society. For example, the tools of production were simple and inexpensive, and their ownership was widely diffused. There was no capital or financial class in the modern sense; business was carried on upon a small scale; the individual was generally his own employer or, if working for another, could look forward to the time when, by the exercise of ordinary ability and thrift, he might become an individual producer. Industrially, society was democratic to a degree which it is difficult for us moderns to realize. The economy of 1800, based upon land and the small entrepreneur with an economic cushion of a seemingly endless frontier, necessitated little if any government planning or regulation. The task of the state was to keep the peace, restrain the Indian, and protect the national security from outside aggression. With external obstacles minimized and with government performing only the most elemental policing and governmental functions, the individual was left free to chart his own destiny, restrained only by his own shortcomings and the accidents of nature. The pioneer was not much interested in legal forms or political theory—his liberty was inherent in the wilderness demanding free and courageous men. His rights were indeed "self-evident." He wanted and needed only to be left alone to his work. As pointed out by J. Allen Smith in his famous book *The Spirit of American Government*, the degree of individual freedom and the initiative which a community may enjoy is not wholly or even mainly a matter of constitutional forms. The actual liberty of the individual may vary greatly without any change in the legal or constitutional organization of society. The control exercised over the individual directly by the government may as a matter of fact be slight in comparison with that which is exercised through the various agencies which control the economic society.[2] In this statement we sense one of the problems concerning the definition of individualism and liberty. In other words, it may be possible for the individual to be more free through application of governmental regulation than through the absence of governmental interference. The method seems to be that of balancing pressures or privileges so that the individual citizen, under the impact of economic or social restriction, may be freed by governmental interference easing the restrictions of economic and social forces. It should be noted that the theory of laissez faire was advocated by the masses of the people when, having little or no political power, they sought to restrain the control of the ruling privileged classes. The history of political development demonstrates that as the franchise was extended and as the people gained political control there has been a tendency toward the more extensive use of the power of government. In other words, democratic government was made responsive to the needs of the community. The so-called inalienable rights of life, liberty, and the pursuit of happiness are recognized as not self-enforcing. The measure of their protection will frequently depend upon the number of people who have a material as well as spiritual interest in their preservation. To utilize one of the bitterest ironies of Anatole France, the establishment of the equal rights of rich and poor to sleep under bridges is not merely guaran-

2 J. Allen Smith, *The Spirit of American Government* (New York: Macmillan Co., 1907), 303.

teed. These rights must be redefined in terms of the present. This is the challenge of progressive politics.

Liberty may have two aspects—one negative, the other positive. One does not speak of liberty at all unless there is a disposition to perform an act. Given such a disposition, negative liberty implies an external obstacle. With such an obstacle in mind, negative liberty means merely its absence or removal. Thus, in an age of religious zeal, negative liberty will mean freedom from an oppressive church; when men seek to have self-government, they covet liberty from a tyrannical state; when they are ambitious to rise in the economic scale, negative liberty will mean escape from the limitation and inequalities imposed by the existing industrial hierarchy. Negative liberty plays an unimportant part in the lives of apathetic men. But to those persons of democratic faith aspiring to new goals and new heights, the removal of restraint releases a compelling force.

Positive liberty means that an externally unimpeded interest is capable of proceeding to its realization.[3] In other words, positive liberty embraces not only the removal of restraint but also the arrangement of all factors so as to make accomplishment possible. If it is the function of government to promote the orderly and compatible liberties of men, this function must be extended to embrace positive and not merely negative liberties. It is not enough that both the rich and the poor may sleep under bridges. The rich need not and will not; the poor must and shall if negative liberty is all that is guaranteed. With this thought in mind, Mr. Roosevelt and his associates feel that the most

[3] Richberg, "Constitutional Aspects of the New Deal," 26.

ancient, persistent, and oppressive enemies of liberty are
not always external hindrances, whether physical or human,
but are poverty and ignorance, insecurity and fear. Thus,
an attempt made for a better distribution of wealth and the
maintenance of at least a subsistence by work relief programs, such as the Works Progress Administration
(W.P.A.), what government does in the way of education,
public information, housing, health, increased wages and
reduced hours of labor, or the redistribution of wealth,
may be as much a service of liberty as the protection of
man against external interference. It would be misleading
to think that there is any clear line of demarcation between
liberty and welfare. "Even the most fanatic adherent of
the doctrine that 'that government is best which governs
least,' must admit that there is, always has been, and must
remain an irreducible minimum of government function
and that minimum includes protection and safeguard of
human life. We must all agree that actually security and the
protection of liberty is the essence and the power and function of the society." [4] It was with this thought in mind that
the New Deal proponents felt a government not clever
enough to prevent starvation through economic control
could not command the faith and loyalty of its citizens.
From the beginning of organized society, a government
has never been conceded the right to demand allegiance of
the citizen or subject except as such government could and
would protect the society or its members from dangers
against which they could not protect themselves. The matter of the government being able to afford adequate pro-

[4] Ickes, *The New Democracy*, 38.

tection to the society may not always involve the restrictive use of tangibles but may also include regulation of such intangibles as an economic system. The New Deal exponents have adhered to this economic interpretation of political democracy. Their study of economic and political history leads them to believe that absence of government control in a society of relative economic equality is democratic and conducive to individual freedom. However, when such an intangible force as an economic system upsets the balance of relative equality, then, if government be democratically controlled, the state must interfere in order to restore the balance. President Roosevelt's words in his famous Commonwealth Club speech are characteristic of the New Deal attitude: "We know that liberty to do anything which deprives others of those elemental rights is outside the protection of any compact; and that Government in this regard is the maintenance of a balance, within which every individual may have a place if he will take it; in which every individual may find safety if he wishes it; in which every individual may attain such power as his ability permits, consistent with his assuming the accompanying responsibility." [5]

One would not be in error in stating that for the New Dealers the essence of a liberal society is that it makes the common good available not only to a privileged class but to all in so far as the capacity of each permits him to share it. The aim of such a society is to release man's inherent powers and capacities so that the individual can contribute

[5] Franklin D. Roosevelt, Commonwealth Club speech, San Francisco, September 23, 1932, in *The Public Papers and Addresses*, I, 755.

to the common good. Freedom or liberty does not consist only in the absence of restraint but also in a positive power or capacity of doing or enjoying something worth doing or enjoying. If restraints or obstacles are removed, the task is performed in the conviction that the individual freed from restraint will move on to develop and prosper. Thus in the attempt to reform and regulate the economic organization of the American community, the New Deal has sought to equalize privileges by curbing here and adding there. Harking back to the political program of Theodore Roosevelt, the New Dealers were convinced a democracy can be such in fact only if there is some rough approximation to similarity in stature among the men composing it—a simple and poor society can exist as a democracy on the basis of sheer individualism, but a rich and complex society cannot so exist; for some individuals, and especially those artificial individuals called corporations, become so very big that the ordinary individual is utterly dwarfed beside them, and cannot deal with them on terms of equality.[6]

Most of the New Deal thought centering around the concepts of liberty and individualism has been concerned with economic institutions. The severity of the Depression with its trail of bankruptcy and destitution came close to making a mockery of abstract political ideals. For the masses of people, political democracy could prove its basic soundness primarily by giving security. Rugged individualism was identified with exploitation and social irresponsibility. The task of government came to be the development of an

---

[6] Theodore Roosevelt, *An Autobiography* (New York: Macmillan Co., 1913), 512.

economic declaration of rights, an economic constitutional order. As President Roosevelt pointed out, "If our present social and political order is to endure, it must prove itself worthy of our toil and self sacrifice and of the lives of those who have been before us." [7] The New Deal administration sought to restore the "confidence that the majority of men and women in this country rightfully repose in their own integrity and ability." [8] Governmental action was to mesh more closely with the rights and essential needs of the individual man and woman. The machine age was to be made to serve the men and women who ran the machines. If modern government was to justify itself, "it must see to it that human values are not mangled and destroyed." [9] Here we see an affirmation of the positive governmental responsibility for public welfare. This is a far cry from the negative liberty of the eighteenth century, but a clear statement of the positive liberty of the modern social democratic theory. Again we find the concept of government responsibility for positive liberty stated: "Let us be clear at the outset that the liberty of individuals to carry on their business should not be abrogated unless the larger interests of the many are concerned. It is the purpose of government to see that not only the legitimate interests of the few are protected, but that the welfare and rights of the many are conserved." [10] Individual liberty, to Mr. Roosevelt, implied much more than restriction of governmental authority. It meant the placing of effective power

[7] Franklin D. Roosevelt, *Looking Forward*, 246.
[8] *Ibid.*, 249.
[9] Franklin D. Roosevelt, *The Public Papers and Addresses*, V, 550.
[10] Franklin D. Roosevelt, *Looking Forward*, 139.

in government in order that it might act as an instrument of social control and social planning. With all the emphasis upon the use of government power for reformed regulation, it would be wrong to assume that the New Deal sought to establish a paternalistic system. The President frequently remarked that any paternalistic system which tries to provide for security for everyone from above only calls for an impossible task and a regimentation utterly uncongenial to the spirit of the American people. What was wanted was not subsidy, pampering, and relief, but an ordering of things so that the individual could exercise his own talents and capacities. Government cooperation or assistance was given in order to make the system of free enterprise work, to provide a minimum of security without which the competitive system cannot function, to restrain the kind of individual action which in the past had proved harmful to the community. As stated by Mr. Ickes, "It is no impairment of liberty and individualism to recognize the rights of others . . . . an individualist can live his life his own way and still be a considerate neighbor and a good citizen. He can be guided by the principle of the greatest good for the greatest number without yielding his individualism or suffering any restriction of his rights and liberties except such restrictions as are reasonable and must be imposed upon everyone in order to assure to all the fullest opportunities of a rich and full life." [11] The same theme runs through innumerable statements of New Deal leaders. The community as a whole becomes the center of attention. Here we see a rediscovery of the community as a

[11] Ickes, *The New Democracy*, 41–42.

corporate body of which both institutions and individuals are but a part. The idea of a collective well-being or the common good underlies any claim to private life. The precondition of the exercise of individual freedom is its relationship to the common welfare. Whereas eighteenth-century liberalism may have identified the common good with an accumulation of separate individual benefits, thereby emphasizing the egoistic nature of the individual, the New Deal sought to temper the idea of rugged individualism with some norm of social responsibility. Mr. Roosevelt clearly stated the idea: "I believe in individualism; I believe in individualism in the arts, the sciences, and the professions. I believe in it in business. I believe in individualism in all these things—up to a point where the individualist starts to operate at the expense of society." [12] Government was to be the judge of the "point of injury." The words *freedom* and *liberty* were "not to mean a license to climb upwards by pushing other people down." [13]

Different people have different notions about the meaning of liberty. Abraham Lincoln used this homely example. He said, "The shepherd drives the wolf from the sheep's throat, for which the sheep thanks the shepherd as his liberator, while the wolf denounces him for the same act as the destroyer of liberty . . . . Plainly, the sheep and the wolf are not agreed upon a definition of the word liberty; and precisely the same difference prevails today among us human creatures . . . and all professing to love liberty." Possibly much of the argument about the New Deal pro-

[12] Franklin D. Roosevelt, *The Public Papers and Addresses,* V, 488.
[13] *Ibid.,* IV, 341.

gram revolves around this analogy. It all depends on whom is being affected and the results obtained. Then too, our thinking in the field of political economy may lag because of the rapidity of social and economic change all taking place within the legal framework of a constitutional system moored to an age long past. There is yet another approach to the apparent contradiction embraced in Lincoln's analogy. Liberty (or its restriction) has always received its meaning in the material well-being of those affected. For those who are impoverished, underprivileged, and denied the opportunity for constructive work, liberty means the right of every man to have a job at wages adequate to support his family in decency and comfort; to educate his children; to give him a modest surplus for the legitimate pleasures and recreation. Liberty means to him protection by his government of the individual for exploitation. Most persons would agree to this statement of liberty if in the accomplishment of the goal, some of the more favorably established would not have to sacrifice or be compelled to give up present privileges and advantages. Yet, liberty is a hollow word if privileges are accorded to some that are denied to others. Possibly the only suitable measuring stick of a continuing definition of liberty is "the greatest good for the greatest number." The students of Bentham and the whole Utilitarian school accepted this principle.

The New Deal became convinced that to the accepted rights of personal liberty, political participation, rights of property, and rights of local self-government, there must be added a series of new rights—primarily economic. First of all, there must be the right to creative work, to profitable and useful employment—profitable not only to the individual but to the community as a whole. This right has been proclaimed by the President as the central principle of the New Deal policy. The right to an adequate standard of living for all persons, measured by the productive capacity of the nation and a more equitable distribution of the national income, is a second basic economic right. The right of the worker, through collective bargaining, to set down the terms of his labor and to a substantial share in the management of the industry to which he has devoted his labor and his life, is a third basic right. Although this principle was hotly contested through the early years of the New Deal, the war emergency has brought the realization and application, if only in a limited manner. A fourth basic right in the declaration of economic liberty is that of security—security against the hazards of unemployment, accident, illness, and old age. The beginning has been made and the acceptance of the fourth basic right is to be testified to by the endorsement of such a social program by all contemporary political parties. The New Deal has suggested, if not applied, a fifth basic right—that of the maintenance of health. The people's health is not to be left to the accident of individual fortune. Already, through various state and federal programs, health protection is becoming a public responsibility. A sixth great right is that of leisure and its effective use. The rapid expansion of community-planned recreation programs is testimony to the growth of acceptance of this novel public service.[14]

These six rights may well constitute the embryo for the economic constitution or declaration of rights of which

[14] Walter J. Shepherd, "Democracy in Transition," *American Political Science Review*, XXIX (1935), 12–13.

Mr. Roosevelt has so often spoken. Surely, they constitute something essentially new in our national philosophy. Yet, they are logical developments of a people experienced in the democratic government attempting to revise and remold political doctrine to an industrial system and contemporary needs. The adaptations and changes of the last ten years in both the economic and political spheres should not be alarming to one dedicated to the principles of liberty, equality, and fraternity or the inalienable rights of life, liberty, and the pursuit of happiness. Democracy is not a mere scheme for the redistribution of wealth. It is fundamentally a theory of social progress. In so far as it involves the distribution of wealth, it does so as a necessary condition or means of progress and not as an end in itself. The new economic rights are likewise not ends in themselves. They are means to an end—individual development. The individual is yet the focal point. The dignity of the individual, however, must blend into a brotherhood, not a jungle. The state has mobilized the collective power of the body politic to assure economic security without the sacrifice of political liberty. A people in control of their government through the processes of election need fear no one but themselves.

CHAPTER 6

In the American Tradition

THE NEW DEAL is America's most recent attempt to secure economic liberty for the average man. It has boldly cast aside any allegiance to the theory of laissez faire and has demanded that government assume responsibility for the welfare of the nation. It recognizes that economic laws are not sacred, unmanageable principles, but rather can be and must be adjusted to changing conditions. It maintains that if democracy is to continue as our form of government, democratic processes must not be restrained by outworn and antiquated limitations. Mere form and tradition must not be permitted to deny government those powers which are essential for the maintenance of social justice. It regards the task of statesmanship as the securing of a balance between all interests. The farmer, the laborer, the industrialist, and the financier—all have necessary functions to perform; the duty of the government is to secure performance and to protect the weak from the strong. The New Deal is no enemy of private property or the profit system. In fact, it seeks to insure the continuance of the established system by the maintenance of conditions which will nourish it. It believes unrestrained concentration of wealth and an ever-growing proletariat to be uncompatible with freedom. With respectful attention to the warnings of the great social philosophers, it regards the "middle state" as the best state, one wherein government rests on a wide distribution of private property. It seeks to define property not merely as land, but as a secure income. The aim of the entire New Deal program has been to make it possible for all people to attain a reasonable degree of security, and security through adequate income. It recognizes that man is not politically free when he is economically dependent. Political liberty and economic freedom must be identified. They are inseparable. The New Deal is thoroughly saturated with cherished American ideals. "Its objectives are security, happiness, self-respect, a decent standard of living for the ordinary man, the idea of generally distributed well-being expressed in the Declaration of Independence." [1] The problem attacked—a wider distribution of the wealth and property of the nation—is the same as that which has occupied the democratic tradition since the days of Thomas Jefferson. The ends sought are substantially those desired by every reform movement in the last half-century. Only the method is more sweeping and the program more highly integrated. Whatever it seeks to do, it attempts through tested liberal traditions, "through processes which retain all the deep essentials of that republican form of representative

[1] Lindley, *The Roosevelt Revolution*, 5.

government first given to a troubled world by the United States." [2] It goes back for its inspiration to the Jeffersonian formula of the right of every man to life, liberty, and pursuit of happiness—a formula which, under the conditions of modern capitalism and industrialism, must include the right of every man to earn by his labor a decent living. Many of its policies and much of its program can be discovered in the Populist and Bull Moose platforms; [3] and in some particulars it closely resembles the New Freedom of Woodrow Wilson.

There is in America a long democratic tradition, a care for and interest in the common run of mortals. This traditional interest in the common man is to be found in Jefferson, Jackson, the Populists, the Square Deal of Theodore Roosevelt, and the New Freedom of Woodrow Wilson. The objective of all democratic reform movements has been to secure economic liberty for the masses of the people. It has long been recognized that political freedom and economic security are complementary principles. In fact, our ancestors in writing the Constitution intended to secure freedom through protection of property. Recognizing that only through economic security can a man be free, they wrote one of the great compromises of political history—a compromise between centralized power and individual liberty. Those who read into the Constitution a guarantee of the freedom of one individual to control the lives of others without responsibility for their happiness

[2] Franklin D. Roosevelt, annual message to Congress, January 4, 1935, in *The Public Papers and Addresses*, IV, 15.

[3] Frederick E. Haynes, *Third Party Movements since the Civil War* (Iowa City: State Historical Society of Iowa, 1916).

forget the primary principle of just government, that power and obligation are equal and compensating forces. When in the exercise of individual liberty, a man acquires physical possessions and economic powers which affect the freedom and security of other men, he has accepted an obligation not to use his powers for the injury of other men.

Under our constitutional methods of self-government, public powers are granted and public obligations are imposed at the same time upon those who, with the incentive of private gain, undertake enterprises that vitally affect the lives of others. So long as men fulfill the obligations which they automatically impose upon themselves, they should be permitted to govern themselves. But when they deny or fail to meet their public obligations, then the government, to protect the public interest and to safeguard the liberties of other men, must enforce the obligations which should go hand in hand with power.[4] This duty on the part of government is imposed in explicit terms by the Constitution. It demands that government be the custodian of the general welfare, and, if the situation demands it, take positive action to secure the common good.

For centuries social philosophers have warned of the dangers inherent in the accumulation of wealth in the hands of the few. A state composed of a few rich and a multitude of propertyless individuals rests on insecure foundations. Aristotle regarded such a state as in danger of perpetual revolution and sought to establish his best state on a base of wide distribution of property. In the minds of many social philosophers among the seventeenth-century Ameri-

[4] See Richberg, "Constitutional Aspects of the New Deal."

can colonists, belief in individual ownership was associated with the general belief in political equality and individual liberty. Much of the later eighteenth-century opposition to the development of industrialism was associated with a fear that manufacture and trade spelled the end of both individual ownership and political liberty. Locke's theory, said Samuel Adams, that the protection of property is a primary end of legitimate government "necessarily supposes and requires that the people should have property." [5] Thomas Paine, celebrated as an extreme opponent of governmental intervention, recommended governmental action to break up land monopoly and check excessive accumulation of personal property in the hands of a few.[6] It is unmistakably evident that those who loved freedom the most were those who sought to give all men an interest in and part of the common heritage. The democratic tradition in America is a long struggle to secure for every man this privilege of property and the liberty that attends it.

The New Deal is bound to this tradition in clearly discernible ties. It has sought to bring about a wiser and more equitable distribution of the national income. It recognizes that the basis for political democracy is economic democracy or the system of widely distributed small property.[7] It has defended economic democracy through its defense of the farmer and the home owner. Indirectly, it is defending economic democracy through waging war on plutocracy, or irresponsible finance. It has guaranteed a

[5] Francis Coker, "American Traditions: Concerning Private Property," *American Political Science Review*, XXX (1936), 17.
[6] *Ibid.*, 18.
[7] Lindley, *Half Way with Roosevelt*, 58.

minimum of economic security through wage-and-hour legislation and the social security program. It has sought to equalize economic power for labor by guaranteeing the rights of labor in collective bargaining and unionization. All of these measures are but a constitution and elaboration of the democratic tradition. They find their historical justification and precedent in the philosophy of Thomas Jefferson, in the progressivism of Populism, the Square Deal, and the New Freedom.[8]

A brief survey of the political philosophy of Jefferson will reveal the essential principles of democratic liberalism on which the New Deal rests. The entire system of the Jeffersonian democratic state is constructed on two basic assumptions, both of which are ethical: that the end of life is individual happiness and the purpose of the state is to secure and increase that happiness. Men, to Jefferson, are more important than institutions, and social good is to be reckoned in terms of human values.

The ultimate end of government, like that of science, of art, of philosophy, is to further the material and spiritual well-being of men. From this it follows that government must be responsible to the people and exist by their consent. Thus, we see that Jefferson, while the supreme individualist, also subscribes to the collectivist doctrine of the greatest good for the greatest number. These are two distinct tendencies in his thought which are superficially incompatible. In affirming the best government to be that which governs least, Jefferson proclaims himself the indi-

---

[8] Berle, "The New Deal and Economic Liberty"; Charles A. Beard, "The Historical Approach to the New Deal," *American Political Science Review*, XXVIII (1934), 11–15.

vidualist and commits himself to an economic theory of laissez faire, but he declares also that the welfare of the whole is the proper purpose of the state and maintains the power of the government to curtail the activities of the individual for the common good. "On the side of individualism, the society must be regarded on an aggregate, the members of which are free to seek their own ends as they see fit. On the other side, the group is an organism; the parts are equal, and are subject to such restrictions on their personal liberty as the health of the organism may require." [9] We have here an organic conception of the society in opposition to John Locke's individualism. The state as a whole, of which the component individuals are parts, and the property rights conceded to each are conditional on their compatibility with the good of the whole.[10]

Having gone so far, one finds it apparent that the individualistic and socialistic tendencies in Jefferson are no longer incompatible. Both stem from the initial premise of the democratic state: that the purpose of government is to promote the happiness of its members. Jefferson saw that this end was impossible without considerable individual liberty; but it is also impossible, he felt, if certain persons or groups through the attainment of economic power are allowed to coerce others for their own profit. It follows, then, that for the welfare of the whole, the state may upon occasion be justified in restricting the activities of the industrialist, the landowner, the labor leader and may impose

[9] Wiltse, *The Jeffersonian Tradition in American Democracy*, 214.
[10] Charles M. Wiltse, "Jeffersonian Democracy: A Dual Tradition," *American Political Science Review*, XXVIII (1934), 844–45.

regulations and control whenever their activities interfere with the rights of others.[11]

In a most profound and interesting article recently published by Charles M. Wiltse we find the synthesis of democracy and state control directed for human welfare. Concluding his discourse on the dual tradition in the philosophy of Jefferson, he reminds us that "democracy, without an admixture of socialism, cannot survive the passing of an agricultural order; for the profits of commerce and industry are too large, and the power they give too great, to be compatible with the ideals of personal freedom and legal equality. If the power of the state must be checked, lest it be abused through sheer love of glory, how much more must the power of wealth be controlled, lest it be abused through the still more fundamental love of gain!" [12] Thus we see that democracy and socialism are alike motivated by the desire to free the individual from oppression and to guarantee to each an opportunity for personal happiness, for self-realization, for practical liberty and spiritual freedom. We may say that democracy is an attempt to distribute political power among the masses in order to prevent tyrannical or dictatorial control and that socialism is a recognition of the fact that political and economic power must be identified. It is this identification that the New Deal has recognized and has attempted to control. The words of President Roosevelt are truly Jeffersonian in their substance: "The deeper purpose of democratic government is to assist as many of its citizens as possible, espe-

[11] *Ibid.,* 841.
[12] *Ibid.,* 850.

cially those who need it most, to improve their conditions of life, to retain all personal liberty which does not adversely affect their neighbors, and to pursue the happiness which comes with security and an opportunity for recreation and culture." [13]

Like all programs of social reform, the New Deal has not consistently followed its declared policy, and its failures and compromises do give ample cause for criticism. But, in its broad outlines, the philosophy behind the program is fairly clear, and it is essentially Jeffersonian.[14] It has merely emphasized the social rather than the individualistic side of the tradition. This has been no mere matter of capricious choice but a matter of necessity. If subsistence homesteads, slum clearance, industrial codes, and public power enterprises are something apart from the usual public or state activities, the New Deal did not concoct such programs out of thin air. They are projects which could not have been blocked much longer. Continued efforts to do so would have invited their attainment through some other, more undesirable form. These projects, and others like them, are not accidents. They are being thrown up by strong forces underlying the political and social development of the country. They imply a reconstruction or a balancing of the old economic processes based upon individual initiative and competition. They emphasize the principle of cooperation and at the same time broaden enormously the sphere in which cooperation may function,

[13] Franklin D. Roosevelt, annual message to Congress, January 6, 1937, in *The Public Papers and Addresses*, V, 636.
[14] Claude G. Bowers, *Jefferson in Power* (Boston: Houghton Mifflin Co., 1936), Chap. 12.

without destroying individual freedom. It may be fairly stated that if the New Deal has laid stress on the cooperative and social sphere, if any sort of a working balance between liberty and equality is to be effected, it has all been done with the purpose of salvaging and then securing private enterprise and constitutional government.

Thomas Jefferson envisioned his democratic, individualistic state based on an agricultural economic and social system. This was his ideal; but realizing the probability of industrialization and concentration of economic power in the hands of the few, he proclaimed throughout his entire political career that property rights conceded to each are conditional on their compatibility with the good of the whole. His Embargo Act of 1807 is exemplary of his policy of social control over property and individuals for the advantage of the whole people. He consistently regarded the functions of government to be broadly divided into productive and repressive actions—the latter being necessary for the preservation of order, the protection of the individual or group from internal or external infringement of guaranteed rights. Productive functions included the regulation and encouragement of agriculture, commerce and industry, public works, education, and in general, all that the twentieth century knows as social legislation.[15] The conditions in the Jeffersonian era necessitated but a minimum of social control, but Jefferson's political philosophy provides adequate expansion of state action for the general welfare and, in that manner, recognizes that popular gov-

[15] Wiltse, "Jeffersonian Democracy: A Dual Tradition," 841. Also see Berle, "The New Deal and Economic Liberty," 38–40.

ernment can never be independent of the social, economic, historic, and religious circumstances that surround it. Where once this was a continent of decentralized economic forces, for which the old political democracy of Jeffersonian individualism sufficed, it is now a land whose industry is concentrated into always bigger and bigger units and where the relations between the banks and business on the one hand and the structure, activities, and procedure of the federal government on the other are the central problems of political life. It is this fundamental change in our social and economic structure that has called into play the second part of the Jeffersonian philosophy—the use of social action to preserve and protect the life, liberty, and happiness of the individual. It is this part of the dual tradition of Jeffersonianism that is so singly displayed in the political action of the New Deal. We may justifiably say that perhaps the most significant feature of the socialized democracy of the New Deal is the acceptance by the state of the responsibility for keeping the economic machinery in operation. The one perfectly clear fact of the modern era seems to be that political and economic power are not separate and distinct entities living in a vacuum, but elements that must and will be identified. The individualistic theory of democracy tended to concentrate political and economic power in the hands of the dominant economic groups, whereas social democracy seeks to work out the problem by abrogating to the state the direction of the economic life of the nation. In the process, "it is inevitable that individual liberty will in certain particulars be curtailed as the activities of government are extended; only by some such means can the welfare of the group as a whole be secured," [16] and the welfare of the group is the end of the state.

It cannot be overemphasized that America had little need of political theories or long-drawn-out treatises on "liberty" and "individualism" during the first three-quarters of the nineteenth century. Ours was a land of opportunity, of expansion, of unprecedented frontier. Our sacred liberties and rights rested less on documents and law than on free land and natural resources. Once the issue of agrarianism versus industrialism was settled by the Civil War, industrial development charged ahead unfettered by law or restraint. To Americans brought up in the tradition that "that government is best which governs least," any form of governmental action for the common man seemed reactionary and downright arbitrary. Business worshipped at the altar of laissez faire, which asserted that business was a self-regulating mechanism, operating under economic laws for the common good, and that the duty of government was only to prevent crime and disorder. In practice this theory had been repeatedly set aside under the pressure of the railroads, shipping interests, and industrial combinations. Business had received outright subsidies, land grants, and consistently rising protective tariffs ever since the Civil War. Political democracy based upon rugged individualism had become a pawn in the hands of finance and industry. Sporadic attempts to secure state regulation by the Granger movement had brought forth moderate railroad regulation and finally the antitrust laws of 1890. The agrarian grumblings finally coalesced into the Populist movement. It was

[16] Wiltse, *The Jeffersonian Tradition in American Democracy*, 266–67.

a movement of western and southern farmers and eastern workers; its main theme was the right of every man to earn a decent living. Failing prices, a rising cost of living, a mountainous burden of debt, and exorbitant railroad rates were the original grievances, and the unemployment and poverty of the lower classes, contrasted with the vast fortunes of a few industrialists, bankers, and speculators, served to fix the lines along which the struggle was to be fought out.[17] Many reforms were included at various times in the Populist programs, all of them designed to place government more directly in the hands of the people and to restrain for the common good the tyranny of unbridled individualism as it manifested itself in the practices of corporate business and high finance. The principal focal points of persistent agitation, however, were the currency system and the restraint on the growing and menacing power of monopoly.[18]

The Populist platform of 1896 was more specific in its demand for social reform than the earlier documents had been. In addition to the older planks calling for a managed currency, government ownership of the means of transportation and communication, a graduated income tax by constitutional amendment, the abolition of land speculation, and the direct election of President, Vice President, and United States senators, the new party favored the initiative and referendum and an extensive program of public works to absorb the idle labor in times of industrial depression. It likewise sponsored a vigorous campaign against the use of

[17] *Ibid.*, 251.
[18] Haynes, *Third Party Movements since the Civil War*, 281.

injunctions in labor disputes and lent its active support to labor organizations.[19] The strength of this new movement in progressive democracy is attested by the fears and horror it struck in the minds of the rich and powerful. It was branded as "un-American" and "socialistic." It was accused of striking at the foundations of the republic and undermining the entire social order. Whatever may be our opinion as to the political and economic soundness of the Populist program, it did give voice to the rising protest of an ever-multiplying group of the dispossessed and disinherited. Its cure for our economic and political ills was the traditional soothing syrup of the old agrarian school—inflation and more democracy. Herbert Croly in his book *Progressive Democracy* reveals the fundamental weakness of the Populist agitation and the related progressive movements.[20] These militant reformers sought to reclaim a lost paradise—the pristine innocence and purity bequeathed to us by our forefathers. They looked to the past as an era of freedom, individualism, and complete political democracy. They saw in the Constitution a government of the people, and in the Declaration of Independence the equality of men and their right to private property in a world governed by the free market and open and fair competition. The reforms proposed by the Populists were but compensatory balances to adjust the economic system back to the "good old days." The spirit of the Sherman Antitrust Act is not to recognize bigness of business as an inevitable development, but to chastize such growth as the work of evil minds

[19] John D. Hicks, *The Populist Revolt* (Minneapolis: University of Minnesota Press, 1931), 314–16.
[20] See Croly, *Progressive Democracy*, Chap. 1.

and a predatory nature. The entire program of monopoly was a ceremony to a decentralized economy. The purpose of bimetallism, cleverly injected into the Populist program by William Jennings Bryan, was not an end in itself, but a means for temporary inflation, as a step toward a "commodity dollar." The party believed that "it was possible to regulate the issue of money as to make it approximately the same value at all times. The value of money, Populists held, ought to bear as nearly as possible a fixed relation to the value of commodities." [21] All of this was but an effort to free the market of restraint and to regain what the reformers felt was our American way of life. Possibly the most significant feature of the early reform was that never once did any of the "saviors to be" thoroughly analyze the nature of the political system established by the "fathers" nor did they seem to understand the inevitability of business growth and concentration. While the Populist reformers valiantly sought to protect the common man, their program lacked vitality because of its refusal to be critically inquisitive as to the true reasons for the economic problems. It selected individuals as the scapegoats and left the institutions of economic life unscathed. However, we must not be too caustic in our criticism. The terrific impact of rapid industrialization and unprecedented concentration of wealth literally remade the American economy. Agrarianism was forced to yield to industrialization but the habits of thought were still atune to the old economic and social system. The cry of the reformer was to recapture that which was lost. Although this may have been impossible,

[21] Hicks, *The Populist Revolt*, 317.

progressive democracy owes an eternal debt of gratitude to those men of humanitarian purpose who challenged the excesses and greed of the new finance capitalism. The people were aroused and the course of the struggle was set. The issue became clear and vital—can political democracy survive and can it master the strength and ingenuity to control the economic power of industry and capital without sacrificing the liberties and freedom of those whom it seeks to protect? It is this same issue that confronts the New Deal and every democratic system of government.

The New Deal owes much to the Populist program. In many respects it is but the latest edition of its predecessor. The financial policy of the New Deal—like many other of its leading policies, such as labor organization, public works, and business regulation—goes back to the Populist agitation of the nineties.[22] Looking toward a more equitable distribution of wealth and to a managed currency, the New Deal administration has altered the gold content of the dollar and has rendered it flexible within certain statutory limits, by authorizing the treasury to buy gold at a price fixed by the secretary of the treasury on consultation with the President. Mr. Roosevelt's statement on the currency question would have sounded remarkably familiar to the Populist of a generation ago: "The United States seeks the kind of a dollar which a generation hence will have the same purchasing power as the dollar value we hope to achieve in the future."[23] Silver, too, had been remonetized

---

[22] Wiltse, *The Jeffersonian Tradition in American Democracy*, 266.
[23] Franklin D. Roosevelt, *On Our Way* (New York: John Day Co., 1934), 125. Compare the above statement with that of Senator William V. Allen of Nebraska as he outlined the Populist Party's objective on

to the extent of authorizing the treasury to keep 25 percent of its reserves in that metal. This is distinctly Populist in its heritage. In the taxation policy, the social democratic emphasis speaks again: "Not only must government income meet prospective expenditures, but this income must be secured on the ability to pay. This is a declaration of favor of graduated income, inheritance and profit taxes and against taxes on food and clothing, whose burden is actually shifted to the consumer of these necessities of life on a per capita basis rather than on the basis of the relative size of personal income." [24] In the field of business regulation the New Deal, like its Populist ancestry, often speaks in the terms of the "good man and bad man." The "economic royalists" are the bad men of today, but unlike early progressivism the New Deal has recognized the fact of big business and seeks to control its practices rather than attempt to break up the large combinations. The National Industrial Recovery Act with its elaborate system of codes is indicative of the new approach to industrial regulation. The President has proclaimed, "We must adjust our ideas to the facts today. We must learn that many social ills can be cured." [25] It is with this call to action that the New Deal steps forth as the practical realization of progressive democracy.

---

the currency question in 1896: "We believe it is possible to regulate the issue of money as to make it approximately the same value at all times. The value of money ought to bear as nearly as possible a fixed relation to the value of commodities. If a man should borrow a thousand dollars on five years' time today, when it would take two bushels of wheat to pay each dollar, it is clear that it ought not to take any more wheat to pay that debt at the time of maturity, except for accrued interest." Hicks, *The Populist Revolt*, 317.

[24] Franklin D. Roosevelt, *Looking Forward*, 105.

[25] Franklin D. Roosevelt, *The Public Papers and Addresses*, IV, 339.

Ernest K. Lindley, Franklin Roosevelt's biographer, has written that "the New Deal was a happy union of the Square Deal of Theodore Roosevelt's progressivism and the New Freedom of Wilsonian democracy." [26] The influences of Jefferson, Theodore Roosevelt, and Wilson merged with Mr. Roosevelt's experience and observation of the contemporary world to form his own political and economic philosophy. Theodore Roosevelt was at the height of his career during Franklin D. Roosevelt's youth and early political life and then, too, perhaps family ties, drawn closer by marriage, heightened the younger Roosevelt's admiration for the dynamic champion of the Square Deal. It should be noted that the progressivism of Theodore Roosevelt is divided into two related phases. In the first administration he contented himself with resounding speeches directed against the "malefactors of great wealth" and looked with disfavor upon the spreading organization of labor. This phase was characterized by a reverence for private enterprise and a restoration of free competition. The attitude of Theodore Roosevelt was typical of the liberal mind of the early twentieth century. He, like the "muckrakers," looked upon the Constitution as a great democratic document that had been put to evil use by greedy men. The startling revelation by J. Allen Smith and Charles A. Beard concerning the American Constitution and its meaning had yet to open the eyes of the progressives to the need of a program of social action. It required the fearlessness of a Lincoln Steffens and a Bob La Follette to revitalize the progressive movement and to point out that the issue was

[26] Lindley, *The Roosevelt Revolution*, 27.

not one of "good men and bad men" in business, but that the economic problem of ever-increasing economic power was inherent within the capitalistic system.

The Theodore Roosevelt of the Bull Moose days was the early New Dealer. It was the Bull Moose program that voiced the spirit of the social democratic state. Its platform abounds in revolutionary phrases that shocked the leaders of finance and corporate interests. The entire platform was a call to positive action by the state to secure for the common man the blessings of life, liberty, and property. "This country belongs to the people who inhabit it. Its resources, its business, its institutions and its laws should be utilized, maintained and altered in whatever manner will best promote the general interest. It is time to set the public welfare in the first place." [27] The Square Deal looked forward to a political democracy that recognized the change in our social institutions wrought by mass production and centralized industry and finances. It finally grasped the glaring reality that the restoration of a laissez faire economy was not only impossible but would be disastrous.

The New Freedom of Woodrow Wilson was the Democratic Party's response to the progressive trend in American politics. There has been considerable argument as to whether or not the New Freedom merely longed for the restoration of the primitive decentralized economy of the early 1800's or whether it was in step with the progressivism of state action and control over economic life in

[27] Quotation from the Bull Moose platform of 1912, in Lindley, *Half Way with Roosevelt*, 384. See Dwight Lowell Dumond, *Roosevelt to Roosevelt: The United States in the Twentieth Century* (New York: H. Holt and Co., 1937), Chap. 4.

order to insure the rights of the people. Mr. Croly in his book *Progressive Democracy* upholds the thesis that the Wilsonian progressivism was that of the muckrakers and the Jeffersonian liberals. His own words are most illuminating on this question:

The divergent economic interpretations which have been attached to progressivism can, perhaps, best be made by considering the differences, as developed during the presidential campaign of 1912, between the progressives who supported Mr. Wilson and those who supported Mr. Roosevelt. Roosevelt progressivism can be fairly charged with many ambiguities, but in one essential respect its meaning is unmistakable. Its advocates are committed to a drastic reorganization of the American political and economic system, to the substitution of a frank social policy for the individualism of the past, and to the realization of this policy, if necessary, by the use of efficient governmental instruments. The progressivism of President Wilson, on the other hand, is ambiguous in precisely this essential respect. The slightest question need not be raised as to his sincerity, but his deliberate purpose seems to have been to keep progressivism vague—with a vagueness that is elusive and secretive rather than flexible. His tendency is to emphasize those aspects of progressivism which can be interpreted as the emancipation of an essentially excellent system from corruption and perverting parasites. His version of progressivism, notwithstanding its immediate forward impulses, is scrupulously careful not to be too progressive, and like the superseded reform movements, poses as a higher conservation.[28]

It cannot be overlooked that Woodrow Wilson was a lover of human freedom. He did enunciate during the campaign of 1912 that the history of human liberty is the history of the restriction of governmental functions. His

[28] Croly, *Progressive Democracy*, 15.

accomplishments while in the office of the presidency were limited to tariff reform, banking reform, and the attempted eradication of monopolistic control over business transactions. It seems to be the view of many progressive critics of Wilson that the President held that by reducing the tariff, "not only is commerce liberated and the competitive system freed from its shackles, but necessarily unjust privileges are abolished. By eradicating any trace of monopoly, or any possibility of organized control over business, and by comprehensively identifying restraint of trade with restraint of competition, the wholesome action of automatic economic forces is further encouraged." [29] In many respects the New Freedom does resemble Jeffersonian individualism. It proposes to contribute to human welfare chiefly by the negative policy of doing away with privilege and discrimination. It harks back to the golden age of our economic and political purity. It does not speak of planning for the future or of a "new order" but rather calls for the restoration of the old order. A few words from his campaign book *The New Freedom* reveal the Wilsonian emphasis: "We are witnessing a renaissance of public spirit, a reawakening of sober public opinion, a revival of the power of the people, the beginning of an age of thoughtful reconstruction, that makes our thought hark back to the great age in which democracy was set up in America." [30] The New Freedom must be remembered not as a feeble effort at social reform, but rather as a recognition of government's

[29] *Ibid.*, 16.
[30] Woodrow Wilson, *The New Freedom* (New York: Crofts Publishing Co., 1913), 12.

responsibility for the welfare of the whole. In this respect
it is similar to the Square Deal and the New Deal and to all
progressive or liberal traditions in American political
thought. President Wilson recognized that we, as a nation,
are facing "the necessity of fitting a new social organization to the happiness and prosperity of the great body of
citizens, for we are conscious that the new order of society
has not been made to fit and provide the conveniences or
prosperity of the average man." [31] Mr. Wilson's beginning
toward the remodeling of the American social system was
tragically interrupted by the World War venture. Constitutional lawyers and political theorists in search of issues
can build numerous arguments demonstrating the differences between the progressivism of Theodore Roosevelt
and that of Woodrow Wilson. However, nothing can obscure the reality that they both used the powers of the
national government to attack social injustices and concentrated private economic power. It is this essential characteristic that serves as the common denominator.

What, then, are the main roots of the political philosophy
of the New Deal? Some of them are by this time obvious:
Jeffersonian Democracy, Populism, the Square Deal of
Theodore Roosevelt, and the New Freedom of Woodrow
Wilson. The appropriateness of this conclusion is indicated
by the fact that many of the achievements of the last seven
years have been, in the words of the President, "the fulfillment of progressive ideas expounded by Theodore Roose-

[31] Quotation from one of Wilson's campaign speeches, in Lindley,
The Roosevelt Revolution, 48.

velt of a partnership between business and government and also the determination of Woodrow Wilson that business be subjected, through the power of government, to drastic legal limitations against abuses." [32] Thus, the New Deal has recognized that in some respects government sits down at a table of partnership with business and labor; but in others, it exerts the superior authority of the police power to enforce fairness and justice as they should exist among the various elements in economic life.[33] It has recognized that security and protection of life are the essence of the power and function of the state. Refusing to be bound by time-worn ideas as to the function of the state, it has undertaken programs of re-employment of the unemployed. It has subsidized housing projects and initiated vast slum clearance projects. It has assumed the right to control employer-employee relationships. It has carried through the principle of minimum wage not only for women and children but for adult men. It has sought to control agricultural production and land use. It has undertaken the job of credit and banking regulation. It has provided machinery for social insurance and a basic economic security. It must be obvious that these measures inevitably trend to result in a more equitable distribution of the national income. Behind this purpose of a more equitable distribution of wealth is the great social ideal of a happier life. It is this same ideal that motivated Jefferson, Theodore Roosevelt, and Wilson. While the programs of each reform movement may differ

[32] Franklin D. Roosevelt, *On Our Way*, x–xi.
[33] *Ibid.*, xi.

as to particulars, the same spirit permeates the whole tradition. The interest of the common man and a desire to insure him against exploitation and economic disaster have impelled great leaders of the people to demand that government assume its responsibility of providing for the general welfare.

Selected Bibliography

BOOKS

Agar, Herbert. *Land of the Free*. Boston: Houghton Mifflin Co., 1935.

Bates, Ernest Sutherland, and Williams, Alan. *American Hurly-Burly*. New York: Robert M. McBride and Co., 1937.

Beard, Charles A., and Beard, Mary R. *America in Midpassage*. 2 vols. New York: Macmillan Co., 1939.

Beard, Charles A., and Smith, George H. E. *The Future Comes: A Study of the New Deal*. New York: Macmillan Co., 1933.

Becker, Carl L. *Modern Democracy*. New Haven: Yale University Press, 1941.

Bingham, Alfred M., and Rodman, Selden. *Challenge to the New Deal*. New York: Falcon Press, 1934.

Carpenter, William Seal. *The Development of American Political Thought*. Princeton: Princeton University Press, 1930.

Carr, Robert K. *Democracy and the Supreme Court*. Norman: University of Oklahoma Press, 1936.

Chase, Stuart. *A New Deal*. New York: Macmillan Co., 1932.

Dennis, Lawrence. *The Coming American Fascism*. New York and London: Harper Brothers, 1936.

Dewey, John. *Liberalism and Social Action*. New York: G. P. Putnam's Sons, 1935.

Dickinson, John. *Hold Fast the Middle Way*. Boston: Little, Brown and Co., 1935.

Dumond, Dwight Lowell. *Roosevelt to Roosevelt: The United States in the Twentieth Century*. New York: H. Holt and Co., 1937.

Emerson, Guy. *The New Frontier*. New York: Henry Holt and Co., 1920.

Farley, James A. *Behind the Ballots*. New York: Harcourt, Brace and Co., 1938.

Frederick, J. George. *A Primer of New Deal Economics*. New York: The Business Bourse, 1933.

Gettell, Raymond G. *History of American Political Thought*. New York and London: Century Co., 1928.

Hacker, Louis M. *American Problems of Today*. New York: F. S. Crofts, 1938.

Hoover, Herbert. *Addresses Upon the American Road*. New York: Charles Scribner and Sons, 1938.

————. *The Challenge to Liberty*. New York and London: Charles Scribner and Sons, 1934.

Ickes, Harold L. *The New Democracy*. New York: W. W. Norton and Co., 1934.

Jacobs, Harold. *Theodore Roosevelt and His Times: A Chronicle of the Progressive Movement*. New Haven: Yale University Press, 1921.

Jacobson, Mark J. *The Development of American Political Thought*. New York and London: Century Co., 1932.

Jaime, Gurza. *Logic, Roosevelt and the American People*. Mexico City: Mexico Editorial, 1935.

Lawrence, David. *Beyond the New Deal*. New York: McGraw-Hill Book Co., 1934.

————. *Stumbling into Socialism*. New York: Appleton-Century Co., 1935.

Lindley, Ernest K. *Franklin D. Roosevelt: A Career in Progressive Democracy*. New York: Blue Ribbon Books, 1934.

————. *Half Way with Roosevelt*. New York: Viking Press, 1936.

————. *The Roosevelt Revolution*. New York: Viking Press, 1933.

Lippmann, Walter. *The Good Society*. Boston: Little, Brown and Co., 1937.

Ludwig, Emil. *Roosevelt*. New York: Viking Press, 1938.

Merriam, Charles E. *The New Democracy and the New Despotism*. New York: McGraw-Hill Book Co., 1939.

Mills, Ogden L. *Liberalism Fights On*. New York: Macmillan Co., 1936.

Peel, Roy V., and Donnelly, Thomas. *The 1932 Campaign: An Analysis*. New York: Farrar and Rinehart, 1935.

Quayle, Oliver A., Jr. (comp.). *Proceedings of the Democratic National Convention*. Washington, D.C.: Master Reporting Co., 1936.

Robey, Ralph W. *Roosevelt Versus Recovery*. New York and London: Harper Brothers, 1934.

Roosevelt, Franklin D. *Looking Forward*. New York: John Day Co., 1933.

————. *On Our Way*. New York: John Day Co., 1934.

————. *The Public Papers and Addresses* (1928–1936). 5 vols. New York: Random House, 1938.

————. *The Public Papers and Addresses* (1937–1940). 4 vols. New York: Macmillan Co., 1941.

Roosevelt, Theodore. *An Autobiography*. New York: Macmillan Co., 1913.

————. *The Strenuous Life*. New York: Century Co., 1900.

Schlesinger, Arthur Meier. *The New Deal in Action*. New York: Macmillan Co., 1939.

Smith, J. Allen. *The Spirit of American Government*. New York: Macmillan Co., 1907.

Spahr, Margaret. *Readings in Recent Political Philosophy*. New York: Macmillan Co., 1935.

Strachey, John. *The Coming Struggle for Power*. New York: Modern Library, 1935.

Swisher, Carl Brent (ed.). *Selected Papers of Homer Cummings*. New York: Charles Scribner's Sons, 1939.

Taft, Charles P. *You and I and Roosevelt*. New York: Farrar and Rinehart, 1936.

Teilhac, Ernest. *Pioneers of American Economic Thought in the Nineteenth Century*. New York: Macmillan Co., 1936.

Thomas, Norman. *After the New Deal, What?* New York: Macmillan Co., 1936.

Wallace, Henry A. *The New Frontier*. New York: Reynal and Hitchcock, 1934.

——. *Whose Constitution?* New York: Reyal and Hitchcock, 1936.

Warburg, James Paul. *Hellbent for Election*. Garden City, N.Y.: Doubleday, Doran Co., 1935.

Wells, H. G. *The New America: The New World*. London: Cresset Press, 1935.

Wilson, Woodrow. *The New Freedom*. New York: Crofts Publishing Co., 1913.

Wiltse, Charles Maurice. *The Jeffersonian Tradition in American Democracy*. Chapel Hill: The University of North Carolina Press, 1935.

PAMPHLET

The Supreme Court and the Constitution. Public Affairs Pamphlet No. 7. New York: Public Affairs Committee, 1937.

PERIODICALS

Beard, Charles A. "Behind the New Deal," *Saturday Review of Literature*, December 22, 1934, pp. 381–83.

Berle, A. A., Jr. "The New Deal and Economic Liberty," *Annals of the American Academy of Political and Social Science*, CLXXVIII (1935), 37–47.

Coker, Francis. "American Traditions: Concerning Private Property," *American Political Science Review*, XXX (1936), 1–23.

Corwin, E. S. "Constitution v. Constitutional Theory," *American Political Science Review*, XIX (1925), 290–304.

Dennis, Lawrence. "Planless Roosevelt Revolution," *American Mercury*, May, 1934, pp. 1–11.

Elliot, F. F. "We the People," *Land Policy Review* (U.S. Department of Agriculture), May–June, 1939.

"Evolutionary Revolution," *Christian Century*, January 17, 1934, pp. 78–80.

Ickes, H. L. "Social Implications of the Roosevelt Administration," *Survey Graphic* (1934), 11–13.

Lippmann, Walter. "Recovery by Trial and Error," *Yale Review*, XXIV (September, 1934), 1–13.

Lorwin, Lewis L. "The Social Aspects of the Planning State," *American Political Science Review*, XXVIII (1934), 16–22.

Lurie, Harry L. "The New Deal Program: Summary and Appraisal," *Annals of the American Academy of Political and Social Science*, CLXXVI (1934), 172–83.

"Mr. Hoover on the New Deal," *Christian Century*, October 3, 1934, pp. 1230–32.

"Mr. Roosevelt and the Liberals," *New Republic*, October 16, 1935, pp. 257–58.

"Mr. Roosevelt's Sermon in Detroit," *Christian Century*, October 12, 1932, p. 1229.

"New Deal Seen as New Freedom," *News-Week*, April 1, 1933, p. 116.

"Notes on Roosevelt's America," *Atlantic*, June, 1934, pp. 654–64.

Richberg, Donald R. "Constitutional Aspects of the New Deal," *Annals of the American Academy of Political and Social Science*, CLXXVIII (1935), 25–32.

"Roosevelt's Speeches," *World Tomorrow*, October 5, 1932, pp. 316–17.

Shepherd, Walter J. "Democracy in Transition," *American Political Science Review*, XXIX (1935), 1–20.

"Toward a New United States," *Christian Century*, March 22, 1933, pp. 382–83.

"What Roosevelt Intends to Do," *Collier's*, March 11, 1933, pp. 7–9.